M

Teach Yourself

VISUAL

Quilting

NOV 3 0 2007

W9-BHS-490

Hakal. 5

Teach Yourself VISUALLY™
Quilting

Visual

by Sonja Hakala

BICENTENNIAL
1807
WILEY
2007
BICENTENNIAL

Wiley Publishing, Inc.

Teach Yourself VISUALLY™ Quilting

Copyright © 2008 by Sonja Hakala. All rights reserved.

Published by Wiley Publishing, Inc., Hoboken, New Jersey

For general information on our other products and services or to obtain technical support please contact our Customer Care Department within the U.S. at (800) 762-2974, outside the U.S. at (317) 572-3993 or fax (317) 572-4002.

Wiley also publishes its books in a variety of electronic formats. Some content that appears in print may not be available in electronic books. For more information about Wiley products, please visit our web site at www.wiley.com.

Library of Congress Control Number: 2007921820

ISBN: 978-0-470-10149-0

Printed in the United States of America

10 9 8 7 6 5 4 3 2 1

Book production by Wiley Publishing, Inc. Composition Services

Wiley Bicentennial Logo: Richard J. Pacifico

Praise for the Teach Yourself VISUALLY Series

I just had to let you and your company know how great I think your books are. I just purchased my third Visual book (my first two are dog-eared now!) and, once again, your product has surpassed my expectations. The expertise, thought, and effort that go into each book are obvious, and I sincerely appreciate your efforts. Keep up the wonderful work!

—Tracey Moore (Memphis, TN)

I have several books from the Visual series and have always found them to be valuable resources.

—Stephen P. Miller (Ballston Spa, NY)

Thank you for the wonderful books you produce. It wasn't until I was an adult that I discovered how I learn—visually. Although a few publishers out there claim to present the material visually, nothing compares to Visual books. I love the simple layout. Everything is easy to follow. And I understand the material! You really know the way I think and learn. Thanks so much!

—Stacey Han (Avondale, AZ)

Like a lot of other people, I understand things best when I see them visually. Your books really make learning easy and life more fun.

—John T. Frey (Cadillac, MI)

I am an avid fan of your Visual books. If I need to learn anything, I just buy one of your books and learn the topic in no time. Wonders! I have even trained my friends to give me Visual books as gifts.

—Illona Bergstrom (Aventura, FL)

I write to extend my thanks and appreciation for your books. They are clear, easy to follow, and straight to the point. Keep up the good work! I bought several of your books and they are just right! No regrets! I will always buy your books because they are the best.

—Seward Kollie (Dakar, Senegal)

Credits

Acquisitions Editor
Pam Mourouzis

Project Editor
Suzanne Snyder

Copy Editor
Carol Pogoni

Technical Editor
Anne McKenzie Nickolson

Editorial Manager
Christina Stambaugh

Publisher
Cindy Kitchel

Vice President and Executive Publisher
Kathy Nebenhaus

Interior Design
Kathie Rickard
Elizabeth Brooks

Cover Design
José Almaguer

Photography
Geoff Hansen

Special Thanks...

To the following companies for granting us permission to show photographs of their equipment:

- Gammill Quilting Machine Company (long arm quilting machine)
- Hinterberg Design (lap and stand hoops)
- Mountain Mist (batting samples)

About the Author

Sonja Hakala is a writer, editor, and book designer. She is the editor of *American Patchwork: True Stories from Quilters* and the author of numerous articles in national publications. She is a partner in White River Press (whiteriverpress.com) and frequently teaches workshops on writing and publishing. She lives with her family on the White River in Vermont, where she quilts, gardens, kayaks, and hikes as often as she can. Sonja welcomes you to visit her website: sonjahakala.com.

Photo by JC Davis.

Acknowledgments

No book happens in a vacuum, and *Teach Yourself VISUALLY Quilting* is no exception, so I have lots of people to thank. First of all, the folks at Wiley Publishing who have been so great to work with, especially Pam Mourouzis and Suzanne Snyder. And my wonderful agent and friend, Linda Roghaar. To the guys of Quilters Treasure in Rindge, New Hampshire, for samples of their hand-marbled fabric. To Sue Wheeler, who got me started quilting and—with her husband, Dick Dumez—allowed us to invade their house for a photo shoot. Sue did the painting in Chapter 4 and let me borrow her pillows for the quilt gallery. To Carrie Fradkin, who let me borrow her mosaic vase and books out of her library and gave me some valuable teaching advice. To Nancy and Buzz Barr, owners of the Country Quilters Emporium, and their terrific staff for answering my questions and letting us interfere with their business for a photo shoot. To Barbara Vallone, who finished three quilts in less than two weeks so I could have them photographed. To Nellie Pennington for sharing her wedding quilt and helping me contact members of the Northern Lights Quilters Guild—Marilyn Mason, LaVonne Batalden, Kathi Moreno, Joyce Lundrigan, Ruth Ann Glick, and Linda Buzzell. To Dori Galton for her lovely red-and-blue quilt. To Vivian Moore, who let me borrow a quilt and introduced me to the Ladies Circle in Pomfret, Vermont. And to the ladies of the Circle themselves: Betty Stetson, Elaine Chase, Miriam Desmond, Gerda Gaetgens, Laura Lee Kent, Barbara Gilbert, and Jean Conklin. To the town of Pomfret, Vermont, for allowing us to use its beautiful town hall, to the staff and trustees of the charming Tunbridge, Vermont, public library, and to Euclid Farmer, president of the Tunbridge Worlds Fair, for allowing us to use their locations for photographs. To my friend Lauren Sherman for her helping hands. To my friend and patient photographer Geoff Hansen, who helped to get the 649 pictures in this book done and done well. To my son Jesse, who cooked dinner, shopped, and helped out while I was on deadline. To my extended family and friends for their understanding and encouragement.

But most of all, I want to thank my husband, JC Davis, for listening to me, for critiquing my work (yes, he is a brave man), for bringing me cups of tea, for making me laugh and putting up with me under stress, and being just the most wonderful guy on the planet. This book is dedicated to him with love.

Table of Contents

 **chapter 1** **Introduction to Quilting**

chapter 2 **Fabric, the Quilter's Medium**

chapter 3 Quilting Tools

chapter 4 Choose Fabrics for Your Quilt

chapter 5 Prepare and Cut Fabric for Your Quilt Top

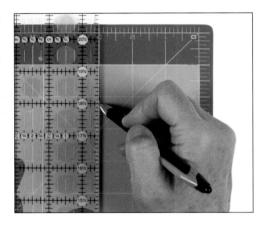

chapter 6 Cut and Sew a Place Mat of Squares

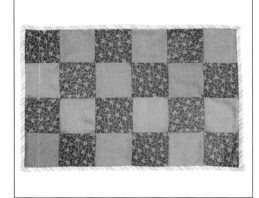

chapter 7   Use Squares to Construct a Baby Quilt

chapter 8   Work with Rectangles: Broken Bricks Pattern

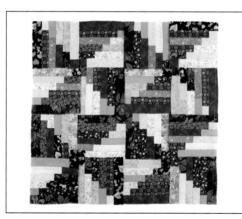

chapter 11 — More Piecing Techniques

chapter 12 — Four Patch and Nine Patch

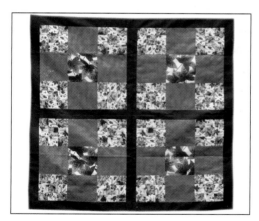

chapter 13 | Triangles

chapter 14 | Joining Blocks Diagonally: Setting on Point

chapter 15 Crazy Quilting and String Piecing

chapter 16 Backing, Batting, and Basting

chapter 17

Tying and Quilting

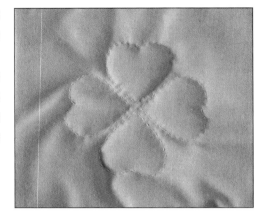

chapter **18** Binding

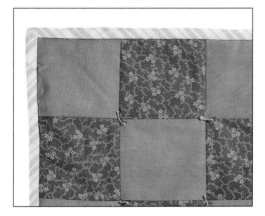

chapter 1

Introduction to Quilting

At its simplest, a *quilt* is two pieces of fabric sewn together with a layer of batting between them. It is an ancient technique, practiced all over the world. Evidence of quilting has been found among Egyptian artifacts and in Buddhist temples located along the Silk Road trade routes that once stretched from the Middle East to China. In medieval Europe, quilting protected knights from the roughness of their armor. In cold climates, women quilted their petticoats for extra layers of warmth. At night, their children slept under thick quilts stuffed with wool.

Until the early 1800s the majority of quilts in this country were made of whole cloth, not scraps of fabric. But the introduction of factory-made cloth in the 1820s and then the sewing machine in the 1840s made it possible for women to make their families' clothes at home. Their leftover fabric scraps were used to make patchwork quilts.

Quilting is still one of the most popular crafts practiced around the world, and the variety of quilts and quilting techniques is staggering. The focus of this book is on the essential techniques you need to start your own quilting adventures. This chapter provides you with the basic concepts of quilting and an overview of the quilting process. Once you've mastered these techniques and understand the basics of the craft, I encourage you to step out with confidence to explore the breadth of the entire quilting universe. The opportunities to experience beauty through this craft are nearly endless.

The Parts of a Quilt

Quilts are built like jigsaw puzzles, one piece at a time. They are a fascinating blend of pattern and color, and are as individual as the people who make them. Your quilts won't look exactly like mine because you have your own sense of color and design, and that's the way it should be. Let's start by learning the parts of a quilt. Each of these terms is explained in further detail in this book but a quick overview is helpful.

Welcome to the quilting universe. I hope you stay for a long time.

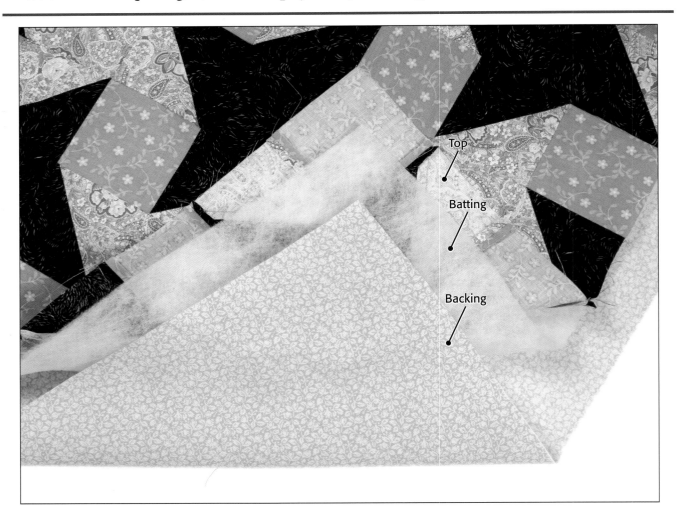

Top

Batting

Backing

THREE LAYERS OF A QUILT

See the photo on the previous page, which shows the three layers described here.

- **Top.** A quilt top like the one on this page is created by stitching small pieces of fabric together in distinctive patterns. The result is called *patchwork.* The process is called *piecing.*
- **Batting.** This is the middle layer of a quilt. It can be made of cotton, wool, or polyester.
- **Backing.** The backing is the bottom layer of a quilt sandwich.

PARTS OF A QUILT TOP

- **Blocks.** Patchwork quilt tops are made in small units called blocks. A block pattern dictates the sizes and shapes of fabric used by a quilter. There are hundreds of different block patterns to choose from.
- **Sashing.** Sashing is the border around an individual block.
- **Posts.** Posts are squares of accent fabrics used at the junctions of two pieces of sashing.
- **Borders.** Borders surround the elements of a quilt top and function as a frame. Quilts can be made with or without borders.
- **Binding.** This is a doubled strip of fabric sewn around the outside edge of a quilt. It is the last step in the quilting process.

THE ESSENTIAL SHAPES OF PATCHWORK

- Squares are the simplest and most basic of all the shapes used in patchwork.
- Rectangles appear in nearly every patchwork quilt and are an essential part of many block patterns.
- Triangles add visual excitement to a quilt top. They are a bit more complicated to work with than squares or rectangles but their versatility is worth the effort.

Most quilters begin a new project with the same sequence of steps. Quilters choose a block pattern, pick out the fabrics they want to use in the block, cut the fabric according to the pattern, and then sew the pieces together. *Block patterns* are the instructions a quilter uses to cut and sew pieces of fabric in a particular arrangement. Then the blocks are sewn together to create a quilt top.

PIECING

Patchwork quilt blocks are made by cutting fabric into certain shapes and sizes. These shapes, in turn, are stitched to one another in an order dictated by the block pattern the quilter has chosen.

Note: *The process of cutting and sewing units of fabric together for patchwork is called piecing.*

Shown here is a diagram of a block pattern called Ohio Star. It is made of nine individual units—a square in the center and in each corner interspersed with four units containing four triangles. The letters in the diagram indicate pieces of fabric of the same size, shape, and fabric. The shading of the diagram indicates places where the same fabric is used in the construction of the block.

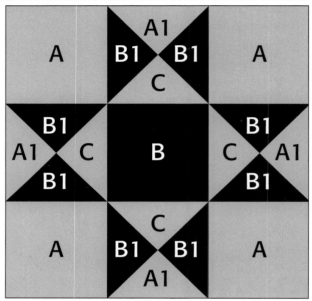

ARRANGE FABRICS

Notice that the block pattern diagram (shown above) is shaded. This shading indicates how the fabrics need to be arranged to make the individual block pattern work. As you will learn in Chapter 4, successful quilt tops and blocks depend on the *contrast*—differences in color— among fabrics selected to make a block. The differences among the three fabrics shown here are quite clear. Compare the above block pattern diagram with the photos of the finished Ohio Star block using these fabrics on the opposite page. Notice how the fabric placement in the finished blocks reflects the shading in the diagram. Also note how the same three fabrics can be rearranged to make blocks that look quite different from one another.

CUT AND JOIN FABRIC

This photo shows the fabrics cut into the shapes indicated by the Ohio Star block pattern. When sewing the block together, the triangles are joined to one another first. Then, working from left to right, the units of each row are joined to one another. Once the three rows are complete, they are sewn to one another.

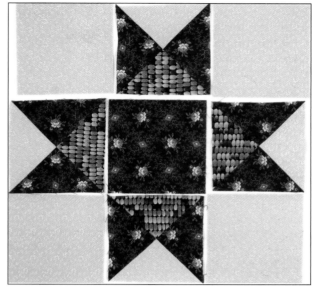

A COMPLETE BLOCK

The fabric pieces have been sewn to one another to complete an Ohio Star block. Note that the four triangle units are turned so that the corn print fabric always abuts the center square.

The Essential Shapes in Patchwork

When you sew scraps of fabric to one another, it's called *patchwork*. Squares, rectangles, and triangles are the most common shapes used in patchwork.

We often hear the words *patchwork* and *quilt* together, but they are not quite the same. A quilter creates patchwork when she stitches small pieces of fabric to one another in a specific pattern. This technique, though it did not originate in this country, is most often associated with American quilts.

The **square** is the simplest shape to use in a quilt. Squares can be cut from all sorts of scrap cloth and sewn together randomly, or you can choose to repeat fabrics to achieve a particular design.

Just because the square is simple doesn't mean a quilt top made of squares must be simple. The square is a great candidate for playful color and design combinations.

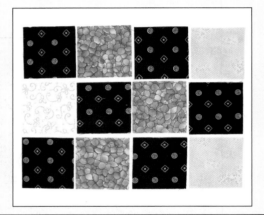

The **rectangle** is the second staple of quilting patterns. Its versatility makes it a welcome addition to nearly every quilt.

Rectangles, such as the ones in this variation of the Log Cabin block, are created by cutting fabric into strips with a rotary cutter, sewing strips of different fabric together to create a *strip set,* and then cutting strip sets into particular shapes.

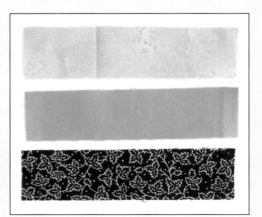

Because they are three-sided instead of four-sided, **triangles** can be something of a challenge to handle successfully. But they add visual excitement to a quilt pattern.

The number of block pattern possibilities, such as this Pinwheel Star block pattern shown here and the Flying Geese block pattern shown below, become nearly endless when you add triangles to squares and rectangles.

Is *block pattern* the term used to describe traditional quilting patterns? Or is it used to describe any quilting pattern?

The real answer to this question is *both.* But most of the time, and especially for the purposes of this book, a block pattern describes a traditional quilting pattern.

There are three different levels of pattern possible in a quilt top. The first level is the patterns or prints and colors in the fabrics themselves. The second level is the arrangement of the individual pieces of fabric in a block. The third level is the arrangement of blocks in a top.

You wouldn't put all these fabrics together in the same blouse. It would be strange to make one sleeve dark and the other light. But you could put all these fabrics right next to one another in a quilt.

Quilt blocks take advantage of the differences among colors and the contrast between dark and light fabrics to create a pattern that combines very different fabrics in a pleasing way.

When you put quilt blocks together, they create a secondary level of pattern that brings the whole quilt top together visually. You can combine the same blocks in different ways to create different patterns, like these log cabin blocks and the ones to the right.

There are over 150 variations of the Log Cabin pattern. Each Log Cabin variation takes advantage of contrast to create an overall pattern in a quilt top. The fun of quilting lies in exploring all the possibilities.

Even though a quilt's top draws the most attention, it's just the first step of making a full quilt. Many quilt tops are framed by a border. Then fabric is chosen for the backing. Finally, a layer of batting adds the warmth to the quilt.

BORDER AS FRAME

Some quilters add borders to their quilt tops. Some do not. A quilt border frames a quilt top the same way pieces of wood frame a picture you hang on a wall. Visually, a border holds the elements of a quilt top together like the border on this Fence Rail quilt.

BORDER AS DESIGN ELEMENT

A border can be made of one fabric like the one at left. Or it can be made of several fabrics like the border featured below. In addition to framing a quilt top, a border can add another design element to a quilt.

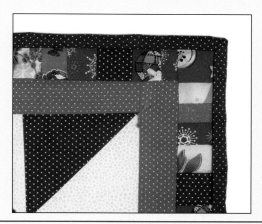

BACKING

In the past, most quilts were backed by plain, unbleached muslin because the back of a quilt was not meant to be seen. But with so many fabrics to choose from nowadays, many quilters prefer to back their quilts with something more colorful.

BATTING

The warmth of a quilt comes from insulating materials called *batting* that lie between a quilt top and its backing. Originally quilts were stuffed with wool or cotton, and these are still popular batting materials. There are also polyester and polyester blends available for batting.

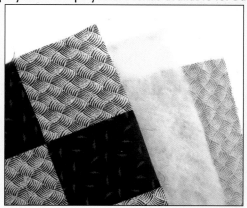

Once a quilt's top is complete, the backing is cut, and the batting is layered between the two. Then it's time to finish the quilt.

QUILTING

The process of *quilting* is when you stitch the three layers of a quilt together to secure them and to hold the batting in place. Quilting can be done by hand or machine. Stitching can follow the straight lines in a block like this *outline stitching.* Please see Chapter 17 for more information about quilting.

Stitching can also be done in any number of fancy patterns that enhance the design and fabric in a quilt top. Please see Chapter 17 for more information about quilting and stitch patterns.

TYING

Instead of quilting, many quilters choose to tie the three layers of their quilts together. *Tying* serves the same function as quilting; it holds the three layers of a quilt together and secures the batting in its proper place. The material used to tie a quilt can be chosen to blend in with the fabric or you may choose a different color to add a design element to a finished quilt. Please see Chapter 17 for more information about tying a quilt.

BINDING

Once all three layers of a quilt—the top, batting, and backing—are quilted or tied together, a narrow strip of doubled fabric is sewn around the outside of the quilt to hide its raw edges. *Binding* a quilt is the last step in the quilting process. For more information about binding, please see Chapter 18.

2

Fabric, the Quilter's Medium

Sculptors have clay, painters have watercolors, and quilters have fabric to express themselves. Fabric is color. Fabric is texture. Fabric can stir up memories of a beloved family member. It can excite us. It can soothe us.

Every quilter falls in love with fabric, and with the current popularity of quilting, more exciting fabrics are available today than at any previous time. But what fabrics are the best ones for quilting? What's the best way to build a fabric collection that inspires you to cut and sew? What do you need to know about fabric before you begin quilting? This chapter gives you a working knowledge of the fabric universe.

Fabric Basics

If you visited a grocery store for the first time, it would be helpful to know that we buy flour by the pound, milk by the gallon, and bread by the loaf. Like these common groceries, fabric has its own set of standards by which it is bought and sold. Understanding these basics enhances your fabric-buying experience.

FABRIC CHOICES

Quilters use every type of fabric imaginable, from polyester to wool to satin and silk in their projects. But high quality, 100 percent cotton is the best for quilting. Cotton fabric wears well, holds a seam, can be washed and ironed, and feels good against the skin. As you shop, look for fabrics that have a firm weave, not too tight and not too loose. A very tight weave is difficult to quilt. A loosely woven fabric frays easily, stretches out of shape, and won't hold a seam very well.

Note: *Try to avoid polyester or polyester blends for quilting. With use, polyester breaks down, forming nubs on its surface known as pills.*

BOLTS AND FABRIC LABELS

Cotton fabric is folded in half and wound around a cardboard center to become a *bolt* (left). A full bolt holds 15 to 20 yards of fabric. A *label* is printed on the edge of the bolt's cardboard center and contains the following information (right): fabric content (100 percent cotton, for example), the manufacturer's name, the fabric width, laundering instructions, and the price per yard.

FABRIC MEASUREMENT

Fabric is purchased by the yard (36 inches) or fractions of a yard such as ½ (18 inches), ¼ (9 inches), or even as small as ⅛ (4½ inches). Generally speaking, cotton comes in widths of 42 to 45 inches so a full yard of fabric measures 36 × 42 inches.

SELVEDGES

The woven edges on both sides of a piece of fabric are called *selvedges.* When you purchase fabric, watch the selvedges as the fabric is unwound from the bolt. If the selvedges dip and bow a lot, this may be a sign of loosely woven fabric that could be a problem in quilting.

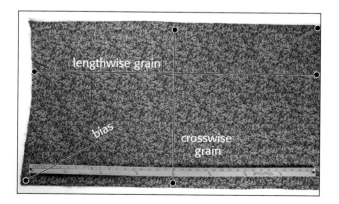

FABRIC GRAIN

Woven fabrics consist of two sets of threads. The ones that run parallel to the selvedges are called the *lengthwise grain.* When cut, this fabric edge has the least stretch. The threads perpendicular to the selvedges are known as the *crosswise grain* (often shortened to *crossgrain*). Cut crossgrain edges have a bit more stretch to them than lengthwise edges. If you cut diagonally across a piece of woven fabric, this is called the *bias.* These edges have the most stretch to them. Most of the time, you cut your quilting pieces on the lengthwise or crosswise grain. But it's important to understand the bias grain of fabric. When you bind your quilt—the last step in the quilting process—you may cut your binding on the bias.

CONTINUED ON NEXT PAGE

RIGHT SIDE/WRONG SIDE

The *right side* of a piece of fabric carries the print of the fabric. It is the side that shows when a piece of work is completed. The *wrong side* of a piece of fabric is the non-print side. Unless the fabric is a solid color or a woven plaid, the wrong side is normally duller in color than the right side. Two pieces of fabric are usually sewn together with their right sides facing one another.

FAT QUARTERS

A quarter of a yard of cotton measures 9 × 42 inches. For many patterns, however, 9 inches is too narrow to be of much use. So quilt shops often pre-cut fabric in a size referred to as a *fat quarter* (a). The dimensions, 18 × 22 inches, yield a better surface area for cutting, and many pattern books show quilts made entirely from fat quarters. Quilt shops often have tables full of fat quarters (b) where you can inexpensively sample different kinds of fabrics.

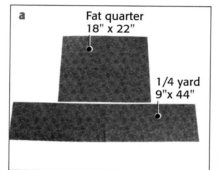

a
Fat quarter
18" x 22"

1/4 yard
9"x 44"

STASH

Quilters refer to their fabric collections as a *stash.* A quilter's stash is equivalent to a painter's set of watercolors. As you continue to quilt, your stash will grow and develop, reflecting your individual taste and preferences. Remember, fabric is your palette, a range of prints and colors that's ready to quilt when you are. As you add to your stash, either through purchases or in swaps with other quilters, try to maintain selections across a broad range of colors, tones, tints, and shades. See Chapter 4 for more information.

Fabric prints come in six broad categories: solids, tone-on-tones, geometrics, floral prints, international prints, and novelty prints. As you build your stash, try to maintain some fabrics in each of these categories. Purchase prints in a wide variety of sizes, too.

SOLIDS

A solid-color fabric is just one color throughout the length and breadth of a bolt of fabric. Solid fabric does not contain any print or color variation. Mixing solids into a quilt top gives the eye a place to rest while it is traveling among the prints and patterns.

TONE-ON-TONE

Tone-on-tone fabrics use slightly different shades of the same color or nearly identical colors in a print. Generally speaking, the slight variations in the color of a tone-on-tone fabric add a bit more visual interest to a quilt than an array of solids.

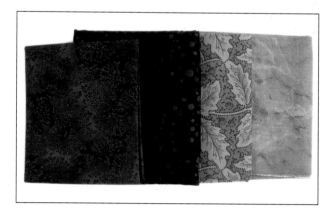

CONTINUED ON NEXT PAGE

GEOMETRICS

Polka dots, stripes, checks, lines, diamonds, triangles, and circles are just some of the many geometric shapes designers use in fabric prints. A geometric print may be a repetition of golf balls or a random sprinkling of bubbles or something resembling swirling paint. Because of their repetition, geometrics hold the eye so they're often a good choice for a border fabric.

Geometrics often adhere to a specific direction in their design. Stripes, for example, are often woven or printed along the lengthwise grain of fabric. If you want to maintain this directionality in a quilt block or top, then purchase more fabric than called for in a pattern.

FLORAL PRINTS

Floral prints include leaves and grasses as well as flowers. This is probably the largest category of fabric prints. Florals may be realistic depictions of their natural counterparts or they may be stylized. When choosing floral fabrics for a quilt, include large and small prints to vary the intensity of the patterns. The variety adds interest to a quilt.

When speaking of floral prints, the term *monotone* refers to florals in only two colors. Since most florals are multi-colored, a monotone print offers the eye a break in the color scheme. Mixing floral prints and geometrics creates visual excitement in a quilt.

INTERNATIONAL PRINTS

The horizons of the fabric world are widening so that it now includes fabric colors, color combinations, and print motifs from an array of cultures. One of the most important groups in this category is Javanese *batiks.* Their color saturation produces vivid tones and their patterns are charmingly irregular. Batiks often have the appearance of crinkled paper, which is a result of the method used to color this fabric.

The international group of fabrics also includes fascinating prints from Africa, folk motifs from Europe, and Japanese kimono prints. Because of their strong colors and design elements, these fabrics create drama in a quilt. They can sometimes be a challenge to use but experimenting with fabric is the fun part of quilting.

NOVELTY PRINTS

While geometric prints represent the abstract world, novelty prints represent something closer to reality. A novelty print may be of race cars or garden vegetables or birds at a feeder or sailboats on a lake or ants at a picnic. Like international prints, novelties can be a challenge to use in a quilt. But they can also be the central element in an eye-boggling design, especially if the print is large. On the other hand, smaller design elements—fabrics with butterflies or bees, for example—often function as interesting borders for a top.

chapter 3

Quilting Tools

Quilting tools range from a needle and thread all the way to a sewing machine with specialized attachments, with lots of helpful aids in between. This chapter covers all of the basic quilting tools for machine as well as hand quilting. As you grow and develop as a quilter, you will probably add to your tool kit, but this list will get you started.

Even if you plan to do all your quilting by machine, there will be times when wielding a needle and thread by hand makes more sense, so it's a good idea to have an array of sewing needles in your tool kit. Add the right kind of pins and a few other accessories for a good start on a great sewing kit.

HAND-SEWING NEEDLES

In quilting, a good starter kit of needles includes an embroidery needle for tying, some short, fine needles called *betweens* (a) in sizes 10–12 for hand quilting, and some general sewing needles called *sharps* (in a size comfortable for your hand) for basting or stitching bindings (b). I like to use a sharp 14 for general sewing.

For sewing machines, use a size 12 sharp for stitching cotton fabrics. If you are sewing batiks, which have a tighter weave, use a size 10 sharp.

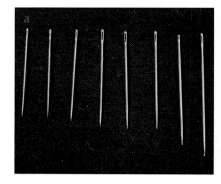
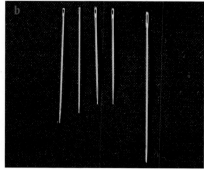

PINCUSHION

A pincushion (or pin holder) is indispensable. They come in all shapes and colors, some plain, some fancy. Choose a pincushion that's firm so that your pins and needles stay upright in it. Many pincushions come with an attachment, usually a smaller version of the original, that's filled with a granular mineral called *emery.* You can clean your pins and needles of corrosion or stickiness by moving them in and out of the emery a few times.

Note: *Consider your sewing habits when choosing a pincushion. Some pincushions attach to your wrist or finger, keeping pins and needles handy, which may suit you better than one that sits on your sewing table. Another option is a magnetic pin holder instead of a pincushion.*

NEEDLE THREADER

Threading a needle, especially one of the small betweens, can be difficult, so you may find a needle threader very handy. Insert the wire loop into the eye of the needle, and push the thread through the loop. As you pull the needle threader back out, the wire loop brings your thread along with it.

Note: Before you begin a long hand-sewing task, such as quilting or securing a binding, thread a number of needles so you don't have to stop in the middle of what you're doing.

PINS

Add a box of quilt pins with beaded heads to your tool kit. These pins are longer than common pins—1¾ inches—which means each pin holds more fabric in place at a time. Also, pins with beaded heads are much easier to grab out of a pincushion or find if they've fallen on the floor.

SAFETY PINS

Safety pins are useful for all sorts of chores in quilting. I keep a small number of large safety pins in my sewing tools to turn tubes right side out, as in the strap for the handbag in Chapter 15. As you learn new quilting techniques, you may want to use safety pins to keep the three layers of a quilt together as you machine quilt.

Good, sharp cutting tools and accurate measuring devices are indispensable when you quilt. When you choose cutting tools, make sure they feel comfortable in your hands. Look for sturdy devices that will stand up to use.

Cutting Tools

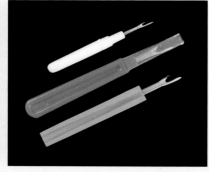

SCISSORS

Over time, most quilters accumulate a number of pairs of scissors. For example, I have a 6-inch pair that sits by my sewing machine to clip threads or cut small pieces of fabric. I have a smaller pair that I keep in a box with my hand sewing tools. The important factor here is that scissors used for fabric and thread should never be used to cut anything else. In quilting, a sharp cutting edge is essential and materials such as paper or plastic will dull an edge after only one use.

SEAM RIPPER

Every quilter experiences a bit of sewing trouble from time to time. When that happens, a seam ripper is usually the best problem solver at hand. The end of a seam ripper is shaped like the letter J with a sharp edge on its inside curve. The extended point is small enough to maneuver between the tiniest stitches without damaging the fabric on either side. Buy one with a cap to cover the point so that it cannot be broken or stab you when you reach into your sewing box.

ROTARY CUTTER

The rotary cutter revolutionized the piecing part of quilting. With it, you can cut longer lengths of fabric more evenly and accurately than you can by hand. You can cut multiple layers of fabric at one time, and as you develop as a quilter, you'll discover a vast array of cutting tricks designed to take advantage of a rotary cutter.

Choose a heavy cutter, preferably one with a self-retracting blade. Rotary cutter blades are extremely sharp so the self-retracting blade is an important safety feature. Be sure to keep a package of extra blades on hand. A dull blade makes cutting fabric a lot more difficult than it needs to be.

Left-handed quilters take note: Rotary cutters are designed so that the blade can be installed on either side of the handle.

CUTTING MAT

When you cut fabric with a rotary cutter, you need a cutting mat made specifically to protect the surface of your work table as well as the cutter blade. Cutting mats come in all sizes. The best choice is 18 × 24 inches with a measuring grid printed on one side. Be sure the grid measures to ⅛ inch.

RULER

The best ruler to use with a rotary cutter and mat is a heavy, clear plastic one measuring 6 × 24 inches. Pick one with embedded gripping surfaces on the back side. These usually appear as small, roughened circles or squares that grip the fabric while you cut so that the ruler does not slip.

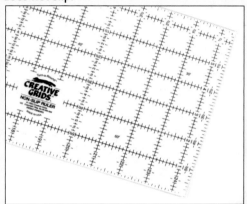

SQUARES

There are many sizes of squared rulers to use with a rotary cutter. These are especially helpful when you straighten completed blocks, cut fabric on the diagonal, or need to cut several of the same shape. A straight ruler that measures in ⅛–inch increments is also very useful.

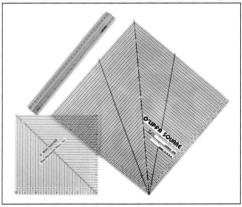

TAPE MEASURE

Tape measures are generally 1 inch wide and 60 inches long. Choose a cloth or plastic tape measure that has measurements marked on both sides, and metal reinforcements on both ends. Retractable, metal tape measures are not a good choice for quilting.

Quilts and quilted projects are made to last, so the ingredients you choose to make them—fabric and thread—should be compatible with one another. When choosing a thread color for piecing, choose something that blends with all of your fabrics. Look at grays, gray-greens, tans, and other neutrals. While you're shopping for thread for hand or machine quilting, check out some of the metallic and multi-colored products now on the market.

There's been an explosion recently in the variety of thread colors available for quilting, including metallic and multi-colored thread. These threads are fun to use in machine quilting, but experiment with them on scraps of fabric to make sure they'll move through your machine properly before you start to quilt.

Note: *Thread manufacturers introduced products known as invisible thread a few years ago. Made of either nylon or polyester, it looks and feels like fine fishing line. It blends in well with fabrics of any color but it is hard to see while sewing. Some quilters believe that monofilament thread causes problems with the tension mechanisms in sewing machines and will also cut the fabric over time.*

As with fabric, you need to read the label on the end of a spool of thread carefully. When you're sewing cotton fabric, it's best to use cotton thread or a thread with a core of polyester wrapped in cotton. Thread that is 100 percent polyester can, over time, act like a knife in cotton fabric, cutting the fabric itself as the quilt is used or washed.

Thread comes in different sizes from extremely thick (size 12) to extremely thin (size 100). For general quilting purposes, size 50 will do just fine. Spools of thread in this size are often marked "general purpose" or "dressmaker." This is the weight suitable for machine and hand sewing the pieces of a quilt together.

Please be aware that there is a thread weight called *quilting*. This is a slightly heavier weight than general purpose thread, and is intended for use in hand quilting. This thread weight is *not* meant for use in a sewing machine.

Your array of quilting tools will probably expand as you delve into this craft more and more. Of all the items described on this page and the next, an iron and ironing board are the most important. Keep this list handy. As you gain more experience, you'll discover the importance of many of these items.

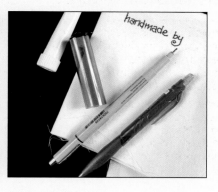

THIMBLES

While the thread-carrying end of a hand-sewing needle is not as sharp as its point, you want to protect your fingertips as you push a needle in and out of fabric. Traditionally, a thimble resembles a diminutive drinking cup made of metal, porcelain, or plastic with a dimpled surface on the bottom that keeps the end of a needle from sliding off. Most sewers use a thimble on the middle finger of their primary stitching hand but some stitchers prefer to use their forefinger. Try the thimble on before you buy to be certain it fits snugly without pinching.

Some sewers, like me, complain that a traditional thimble is uncomfortable. There are now several options on the market including adjustable or leather thimbles as well as small leather circles with an adhesive backing that cover the spot on your finger where the needle jabs your skin. Experiment and choose the one that suits you best.

TEMPLATE MATERIAL

If you want to make a patchwork quilt without a rotary cutter, you will need to make templates to guide your fabric cutting. A template is a shape cut from a stiff material. A quilter uses a template as a pattern, tracing around it onto a piece of fabric before cutting. Experienced quilters tell stories about making templates from empty cereal boxes, and this material or something similar, such as poster board, can still be used. But vinyl templates are far more durable. Vinyl products used to make quilting templates are available in quilt shops as well as in general craft stores.

To learn how to use a template, please see Chapter 5.

MARKERS

Fabric markers come in two types: permanent and non-permanent. Templates are often traced with sharp pencils. Mechanical pencils with HB lead make thin lines which are good for template tracing. Use a metallic, white pencil or chalk marker, available in quilt and craft shops, to mark dark fabrics.

CONTINUED ON NEXT PAGE

IRON AND IRONING BOARD

Choose an iron that has steam and no-steam settings. Many irons automatically turn down the heat if the iron sits still for a certain period of time. This is a safety and energy-saving feature. An adjustable ironing board prevents back strain. Make sure you have a clean ironing board cover, perhaps one that you use just for quilting.

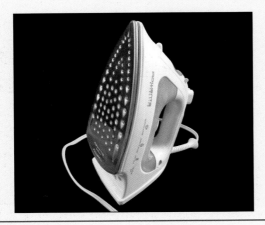

GRAPH PAPER AND COLORED PENCILS

Graph paper is one of the handiest quilting aids to keep around. Use it for designing a quilt or try out your quilt pattern ideas for color and contrast by sketching them. It's perfect for diagrams for projects in progress. Graph paper and pencils are also used to enlarge patterns for hand piecing.

QUILTING HOOPS AND STANDS

A wide variety of quilting hoops and stands is available for the hand quilter. Quilting hoops are wider and of a greater diameter than embroidery hoops so they can accommodate two layers of fabric and batting. For more extensive quilting, try a hoop attached to an adjustable floor stand. This frees up both hands.

Courtesy of Hinterberg Design

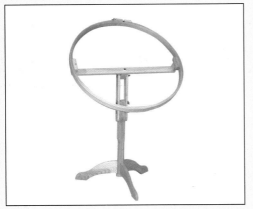

QUILTING FRAMES

If you're hand quilting a large project, a frame is the way to go. In recent years, manufacturers have reduced the size and weight of quilting frames so that they can be taken apart for storage, and then easily reassembled when you're ready to quilt. Some frames are adjustable to accommodate the size of your quilt project.

Courtesy of Hinterberg Design

Sewing machines have come a long way since Elias Howe's treadle-powered invention. Many come with attachments for special types of stitches. Some have a wide array of fancy stitches available at the touch of a button. Some specialty machines are computer programmed to follow any number of intricate quilt patterns. In other words, if you don't already own a sewing machine but want one, you have a lot of choices to make.

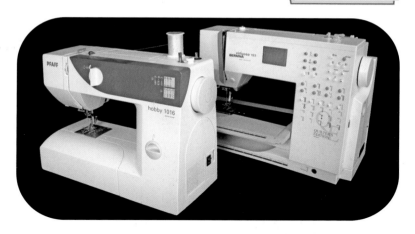

Savvy Shopping Hints

These are the essentials you need in a sewing machine for quilting:

- **Quality tension control.** When you run a seam between your fingers, it should be smooth to the touch if the tension between the bobbin and top threads is working as it should. In some machines, the bobbin thread's tension can be difficult to adjust. Look for a machine with independent controls for the top and bobbin threads.

- **Ease of cleaning and oiling.** As you sew, the presser foot and feed dogs on your machine act like an electric shaver over skin, skimming off minute amounts of fiber from your fabrics. Look for a machine that makes it easy to clean the places where this fiber and lint accumulate.

  Open the bobbin area of the machine to find the places where it needs to be oiled. Read the owner's manual for oiling instructions to be certain you can do it easily yourself. Any machine may need professional maintenance from time to time but you want to be able to oil it yourself.

- **Stitches.** At a minimum, a sewing machine for quilting should make straight seams in different stitch lengths. It should be easy to reverse the direction of the stitching to lock in the beginning and end of a seam. Nowadays, most sewing machines make buttonholes and zigzag stitches in different lengths. While not absolutely necessary for piecing or machine quilting, machine appliqué requires these types of stitches. Plus, zigzag and buttonhole stitching comes in handy for a wide variety of tasks. This option is nice to have in a machine.

- **Operation.** For the best quality seams, make sure your choice of sewing machine can maintain a slow, even rate of speed.

For best results, test a sewing machine before you buy it. Purchase the best quality machine you can. This does not necessarily mean the machine you choose has the widest variety of stitches. It means the machine you choose is sturdy, reliable, and easy to operate. *Teach Yourself VISUALLY Sewing* (Wiley, 2006) is a good resource for in-depth information about sewing machines.

TIP

A sewing machine should be oiled once for every 20–25 hours of sewing. I make a habit of oiling my machine when I refill my bobbin thread.

chapter 4

Choose Fabrics for Your Quilt

Thousands upon thousands of different fabrics are available to the contemporary quilter, from reproductions of nineteenth-century prints to the vibrant colors of Javanese batiks. For the beginning quilter, this abundance of choice can be overwhelming. With so many varied fabrics at hand, how do you pick just the right ones for your quilt?

Quilts are built on the principles of value, contrast, and pattern as well as color. In this chapter, numerous exercises are shown to help you learn how to use these principles to design a successful fabric palette.

Value, Contrast, Pattern, and Color

To many quilters, choosing fabrics for a new quilt project is the best part of quilting. As you learn the fabric concepts and work through the following exercises, remember to keep an open mind about your choice of fabrics. You just never know when that piece of bright orange fabric will turn out to be just the right touch for your latest project.

Let's begin with definitions of the four main terms used to refer to fabric.

VALUE

A color's *value* refers to its darkness or lightness relative to its hue. For example, light colors such as lavender and pink are pale values of purple and red, respectively. Navy blue is a dark value of blue, while maroon is a dark value of red.

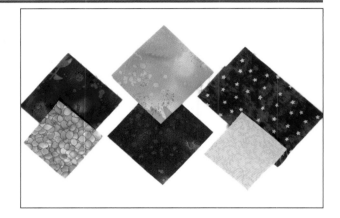

CONTRAST

If you lay a swatch (small piece of fabric) of navy-blue fabric next to a swatch of sky blue, you can easily see the difference between them. Quilters refer to this difference as *contrast.* Your eyes see not only color, but also the differences between such values of color as pumpkin and peach. In a quilt, contrast is as important as color. The contrast between the fabrics in (a) is high while the contrast between the fabrics in (b) is low.

PATTERN

Most quilt tops are made of blocks, such as this North Star block. In turn, blocks are made of individually cut pieces of fabric sewn together in much the same way pieces of a jigsaw puzzle are put together. Generically, quilters refer to the instructions for making a block or putting blocks together for a top as a *pattern* (see Chapter 1).

In addition to value and contrast, quilt tops benefit from a certain amount of repetition among their blocks. This repetition (pattern) fuses the blocks together visually so that instead of seeing individual pieces of fabric, a viewer sees the quilt as a whole.

The Fence Rail quilt in Chapter 9 is an example of how individual blocks in a quilt function together to create a secondary level of pattern in a quilt's top.

COLOR

If you ever have a chance to attend a quilt show, you're sure to hear the phrase "I just love the colors." By and large, people fall in love with quilting because they fall in love with the chance to play with a rainbow of fabrics. Color is fun. Color is delicious. Color comforts us, startles us, and delights us.

As you work with color in quilting, be sure to maintain a willingness to experiment. Sometimes, it's the color combination you thought would never work that leads you to craft an exciting quilt.

Value and Contrast Exercises

The following exercise is designed to help you understand the meaning of value and contrast in fabrics. The human eye naturally thrives on contrast. For example, we are able to read, in part, because of the contrast between the black of type and the white of paper. We thrill to a sunset because of the contrasts among the reds, oranges, and pinks created by a setting sun and the fading blue of the sky. This same principle—the importance of differences among fabrics (contrast)—is a key concept in quilting.

Value Exercise

1. If you already have a stash of fabrics, select 10 different fabrics in the same color family (a). If you don't have a stash of fabrics, gather 10 objects from the same color family from around your home.

2. Now group your fabrics or items together on a neutral surface (something white, cream, beige, or light gray, preferably), and spend a few minutes examining your collection. The color green is used in this example (b).

3. Choose the fabric or object in the darkest shade and place it on your neutral surface. Now, working in a circle as shown or from left to right, arrange the rest of your collection from darkest to lightest. You are arranging these objects in terms of their color value.

Contrast Exercise

1 Picking out the darkest and lightest values of a color in a group is easy. But as you work in the mid-range, the differences in color values become subtler. Choose three fabrics or objects from the middle of the color range in your selection. Separate them from the others. Up close, you can readily see the differences among them.

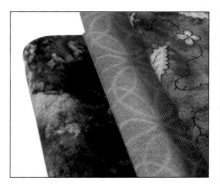

2 Now walk at least 10 feet away from your selections. At a distance, the differences in value are more difficult to detect.

3 When you read the instructions to make a quilt, they often begin with a list of fabrics. The instructions also specify the yardage you need of *light* and *dark* fabrics, because quilt blocks are designed to take advantage of this contrast. Look at the example of a Fence Rail block on the right. Fabrics of little contrast were used to create the block. Because there's little difference among them, these fabrics tend to blur with one another visually.

4 The contrast between the fabrics in these Nine Patch blocks is far greater, so your eyes see the different parts of the block. Notice how five of the nine pieces of fabric in this block are the same, specifically the one in the center and each of the corners. This repetition or pattern becomes key when a group of Nine Patch blocks is put together.

Note: You can test for contrast between two fabrics by sewing a scrap of one to the other. Then step back and look at the result. Can you clearly see the line where the two fabrics meet? If yes, then you know the contrast between the two is high enough.

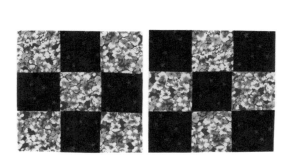

You can choose colors for your quilt in several ways. These color terms will help you develop your color skills so that you can confidently select fabrics for your quilts.

PRIMARY COLORS

In pigment, or dye, the three primary colors are blue, red, and yellow (a). All other colors are combinations of the three primaries. For example, purple is a combination of red and blue, orange is a combination of yellow and red, and green is a combination of yellow and blue (b).

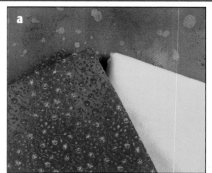

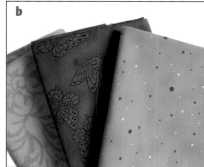

INTENSITY

The term *bright* is often used to describe a color with a great deal of intensity. *Brightness* actually refers to a color's purity. The purer a color, the more attention it gets in a quilt. The fabrics shown in the photo have a great deal of intensity.

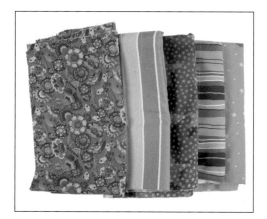

SHADE

When black is added to a pigment or dye, the result is a *shade* of the original color. Brick red is a shade of red while spruce green is a shade of green because they are *darker* than the original colors.

TINT

When white is added to a color, the result is a *tint* of the original color. Pink is a tint of red, for example, while lavender is a tint of purple because they are *lighter* than the original colors.

TONE

When you add gray to a color, it becomes dusky or dull in value. When speaking of color, a *tone* is often described as *muted.* Avocado is a tone of green.

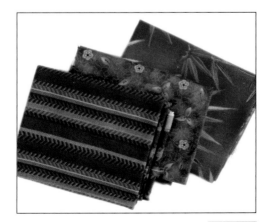

Build a Color Palette

You can use a fabric's print as a guide for building a color palette for your quilt top. Start with a multicolored fabric, one with at least three colors in it. Use this fabric as your starting point as you add fabrics from your stash or visit a local fabric shop to purchase fabrics.

Analyze Your Fabric

1 Quilters often sort their stash by the predominant color in a fabric. Pull some fabrics from your stash, and sort them by color (a).

2 Chances are this fabric (b) would be in your pink pile. Quilters often talk about how a fabric *reads*—meaning their first impression of a fabric—whether it's dark or light, pink or purple. In spite of all the different colors in this particular fabric, it reads as dark pink, and that is how it will function in a quilt.

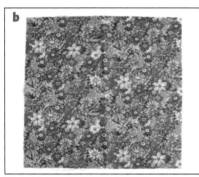

3 Look closer and you notice various tints, shades, and tones of purple, yellow, and green as well as reds and pinks in this fabric. With so many colors, why is dark pink your first impression of the color of this fabric?

First, red is a dominant color and there are three different values of red in this fabric: very pale pink serves as the background for the whole fabric; a mid-range rose color is used in many of the flowers; and a darker shade appears in some of the flowers as an accent, and as the overall color in some of the other flowers.

The next most common colors are in the purple family. Purple is a cool color so it recedes in the presence of a warm color such as red. In addition, purple contains red so its presence gives a visual boost to the various values of red in this fabric. Also note that both versions of purple—a pale lavender and a darker shade that's closer to the parent color—are tones. In other words, gray was added to the pigment that printed these colors so their visual impact is muted.

Three different values of green are in the leaves (a), and like the purples, all three of these greens are tones. This muting of an already cool color makes it recede into the background, especially in the presence of a warm color like red.

Finally, the three yellows in this fabric are so muted that they function as neutrals (b). Neutrals play an important role in quilting because they give the eye a place to rest.

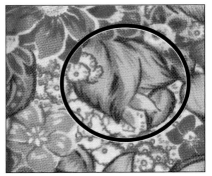

Choose Fabrics

In spite of the presence of two warm colors—red and yellow—the overall impression of the fabric analyzed on the previous pages is muted. In other words, the fabric is tonal but destined to dominate any color scheme because of the presence of red. Let's use this fabric to build a palette for a quilt top.

Build Your Palette

1 For this example, the starter fabric from the previous pages will be in the middle of your palette in terms of color and contrast. Let's begin by choosing a dark color in the red family.

Note: Remember to step away from your fabrics after you lay them side by side so that you can focus on how they read with one another. If you can't step away far enough from your fabric selections, view them from the wrong end of a pair of binoculars.

2 Of these two fabrics in the red family, which one has a value similar to the starter fabric? Place each of your choices next to your starter fabric to determine this. Notice that although both of these fabrics are in the red family, the one on the left is a bright tint compared to the more muted red on the right (a).

3 Make this same comparison with the fabric candidates (b) in each of your color families.

4 Choose some potential candidates for your mid-range fabrics. Bear in mind as you make your choice that your mid-range fabrics need to have good contrast with both your dark and light choices. You want to be able to clearly distinguish among the fabrics in a quilt top. Hold each of your mid-range fabrics next to the starter fabric, and focus on choices that are within the same muted value range as your starter.

5 This process of mixing and matching can take time and may take some surprising turns. Keep your mind open as you choose and re-choose. You'll soon realize that you're developing a palette and that some fabrics seem to suit one another better than others.

6 Line your fabrics up from dark to light against a neutral surface. Step away to view them. Is there enough contrast? Do you like the gradation from dark to light? Take your starter fabric out of your selections. Do they work better without the starter? Remember, until you begin to make your quilt, you can change your mind about any fabric in your selection.

Before you begin your quilt project, it's a good idea to make test blocks from your chosen fabrics so you can check your color and contrast choices. Notice how color and contrast choices impact the Fence Rail examples on this page.

1 This 4-block test uses three fabrics with high contrast. Notice how your eye follows the pattern (repetition) of lines created by the light and dark fabrics while the mid-range fabric is almost unnoticed.

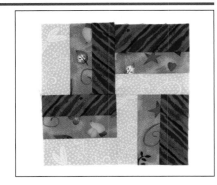

2 Like many quilt block patterns, Fence Rail has a second name: Roman Roads. Unlike Fence Rail, Roman Roads does not use contrast to create a second level of pattern in a quilt top. Its purpose is to create an optical blend of color. See Chapter 14 for an example of Roman Roads.

3 The contrast among the fabrics in this example is low so this combination is not a good candidate for Fence Rail blocks. But this same combination could be used for a subtle blend of color in a quilt top. See the detail of the quilt on page 278 for an example of low-contrast fabrics used in this way.

Quilting and fabric selection heighten your awareness of color and pattern in daily life. Pay attention to your surroundings as you go through your day. You never know when you'll spot a color scheme that inspires a quilt.

This quilt block captures the colors in this selection of flowers and vines in a planter box.

This quilt block was inspired by the colors in the painting.

This fabric selection replicates the colors in this mosaic.

Even though you probably have a favorite color or color combination, part of the fun of quilting is stretching your color horizons through experimentation. A color wheel is the perfect tool to help you do this.

This circular chart was developed nearly 2,000 years ago as a way to understand the relationships among colors. For quilting purposes, use the 12-color wheel developed for pigments or dyes. It begins with yellow in the top spot and works through the *warm colors*—those that are mixtures of the primary colors yellow and red—and then through the *cool colors*—those mixtures that include the primary color blue.

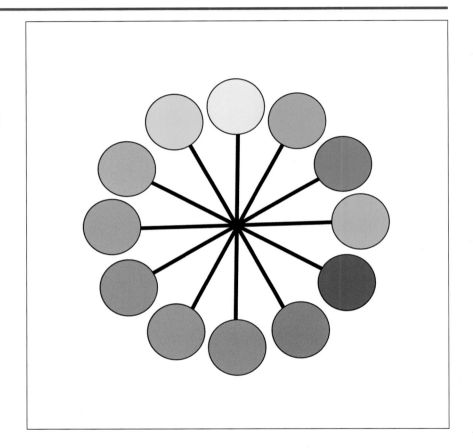

![TIP]

Color wheels are readily available in art-supply stores, and they're handy to have when you're contemplating a color scheme for a quilt. Use your color wheel as a way to experiment with the fabrics in your stash. Start with a color you don't ordinarily use, and experiment to see what sort of fabric relationships you can build with it.

Use the color wheel to set up an interesting color relationship in your quilt pattern. Here are the steps to follow:

1. Choose a color combination from your color wheel. Use graph paper and pencil to draw out your selected quilt block pattern. Using colored pencils, fill in areas of your drawing with color combinations based on your color wheel selections until you find one that pleases you.

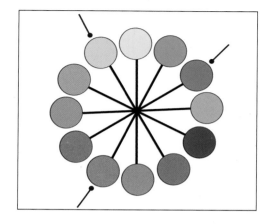

2. Test out pieces cut from fabrics you're considering for your quilt project on your drawing.

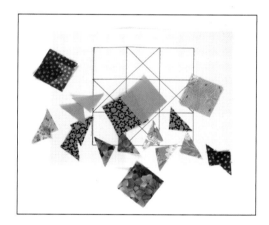

3. When you find a combination of fabrics that you like, make a test block of them to make sure your choices have the color and contrast you envision for your quilt.

Color Relationships

Play with some of the relationships among colors on the wheel to understand how they work with one another.

One Color (Monochromatic)

You can create vibrant quilts using fabric from a single color. Splashes of this one color may be interspersed with fabrics called *quilter's neutrals*—variations of white and beige (the colors you find in *muslin,* a type of fabric). This mixing of a color and a neutral in the same block gives the eye a place to rest. In the Nine Patch example on the right, the color fabrics are mixed with unbleached muslin.

The Nine Patch example on the right uses two fabrics in the same color family.

TIP

Selecting fabric in a store can be difficult, especially if the store is crowded or there's limited space to test your selections. To minimize this, purchase small amounts of your test fabrics—most stores will cut as little as ⅛ of a yard—and bring them home to play with. Be sure to return to the store as soon as possible to purchase sufficient yardage for your project. Popular fabrics don't stay on the shelf very long.

Opposite Colors (Complementary)

When you choose any two colors directly opposite from one another on the color wheel, you set up a complementary color palette. Visually, complements complete one another because each contains the one primary color not included in the other. For example, orange is a mixture of red and yellow, neither of which are part of orange's opposite, blue. Opposites also intensify each other.

Of necessity, a color scheme composed of opposite colors always includes one warm color and one cool. Warm colors, because of their vibrancy, dominate cool colors so a little warm goes a long way in a quilt. In order to lessen this disparity, include a greater proportion of cool color fabrics in a quilt built of opposites (top photo) or use various tints, shades, and tones of the selected colors. Remember, neutrals can be part of this mix as well.

These two examples of Ohio Star squares use the same color combination. Notice how the visual impact of the block intensifies with an increased proportion of orange (bottom photo).

TIP

Remember, quilts last for a long time after the sewing is done so play with your fabric choices until you are satisfied. If you start feeling frustrated, leave your block and go away to do something else. A few hours later, you will see it with fresh eyes.

CONTINUED ON NEXT PAGE

Side-by-Side Colors

Colors next to each other on the color wheel (called *analogous colors*) are usually too close to one another visually to be successful in a quilt top. But three, four, or five side-by-side colors can lead to all sorts of interesting effects in a quilt block. These variations of the Fence Rail block (see Chapter 9) and the Nine Patch (see Chapter 12) use three side-by-side colors.

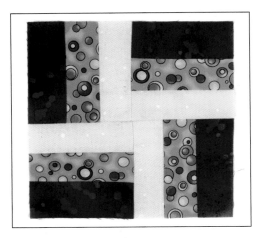

Use Opposites for Spice

Side-by-side color schemes benefit from a little spice. To create this palette, choose two side-by-side colors, and then add the opposite of one of them. This opposite color, used in small amounts, makes a pleasing counterpart to the side-by-side colors. This Nine-Patch block (see Chapter 12) and Ohio Star (see Chapter 13) benefit from a little spice in the center of the block.

Even experienced quilters find it difficult to imagine how a group of fabrics will look in a finished quilt. It's not unusual to carefully select a group of fabrics only to discover that when they're sewn together in a block, the combination just doesn't gel the way you hoped. One of the best ways to solve this problem is through color auditions in a test block. For this exercise, you need two pieces of graph paper, a pencil, scissors, your fabrics, and a glue stick.

① Make two copies of your chosen block pattern in its finished size (without seam allowances). Here is Ohio Star (see Chapter 13).

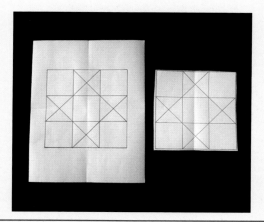

② Carefully cut out the individual pieces from one of your copies. These pieces are temporary templates that you can use to cut fabric for your auditions.

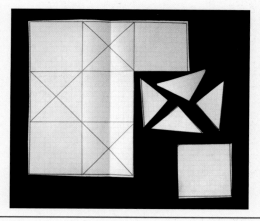

③ Place an individual paper piece on the right side of the fabric you plan to use for that part of your block. Use a pencil to trace around the paper.

④ Carefully cut the various shapes out of your chosen fabrics, and then place them on your uncut copy.

The values of fabrics often change when they sit side by side in a block. Something that seems dark enough for a good contrast suddenly looks muted or a light fabric you were calling pale yellow now looks like pale gold. This is a normal part of the trial-and-error process of auditioning fabrics. Some questions to ask as you audition fabrics are below.

① Does the design of the block show up or is it fading into the background? If the fabric is fading (left), try a fabric with more contrast to the background (right).

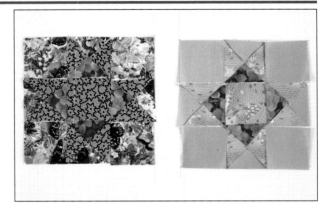

② Do too many of the fabrics look the same? If all the chosen fabrics are florals (left), then the similarity can cause design problems. Alter the print size or add a geometric print to the block (right).

TIP

Vary the size of the prints in the fabrics you choose to add interest to your quilt. Mix large prints and small, solids and abstracts for more visual interest.

③ Does more than one fabric fight to dominate the block (left)? Try using a shade or
tint of one of them to fix this problem
(right).

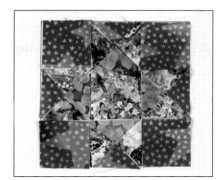 

④ When you fill in your block, glue the pieces in place, pin
it to the wall, and view it from 10 feet away. Do you like it?
If you change fabrics, glue the new fabric over the fabric
you want to replace.

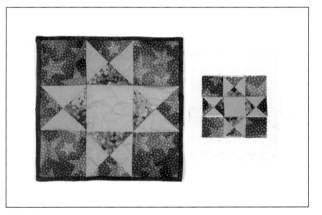

chapter 5

Prepare and Cut Fabric for Your Quilt Top

Every quilt top begins with the same two steps: Prewash your fabric and cut it according to a selected pattern.

Fabric manufacturers commonly add chemicals to finished cloth to prevent mildew and resist soiling. Some people are allergic to these additives while others find them irritating to the skin. Prewashing your fabric according to the instructions included in this chapter not only removes these potential problems, it also pre-shrinks your fabric before it's part of a quilt. You also learn how to test your fabric for colorfastness.

Once your fabric is prewashed and dried, you're ready to begin cutting it for a quilt top. Two methods of cutting fabric for a quilt top are by hand with scissors or by rotary cutter. This chapter includes instructions for both methods.

Prewash
Your Fabric

Some quilters do not prewash their fabrics. This is fine if a finished quilt won't ever be laundered. But for quilted projects—such as place mats or a bed covering that your cat likes to sleep on—your work will eventually need to be washed. So, testing your fabrics for colorfastness and then prewashing them is a good idea. Here's how.

Prewash Small Fabric Pieces

1 If your fabric piece is ¼ yard or less, fill a container with warm water (no detergent), and place the fabric in the water. Watch to see if the water changes color. If it does, drain the water, and rinse the fabric again. Repeat this step until the water is clear. Treat small pieces of fabric gently because excessive agitation can ravel their edges or pull them out of alignment.

2 Once the rinse water is clear, gently squeeze excess water from the fabric.

3 Tumble in the dryer on low or hang on a rack until the fabric is just damp. Iron the fabric smooth. Dark-colored fabrics are more apt to bleed than light, but testing all fabrics is a good idea.

Note: *Prewashing is also important because cotton shrinks approximately 1½ to 3 percent during the laundering and drying process. This shrinkage can have an adverse impact on a finished quilt.*

Do not test your fabrics for colorfastness in a plastic tub. Excess dye stains plastic. Use a metal, glass, or ceramic container.

Prewash Large Fabric Pieces

1 If you have a piece of fabric measuring ½ yard or more, test it for colorfastness by cutting a small swatch from it. Place the swatch in warm water in a glass, and watch to see if the water stays clear. If the fabric bleeds, test it again after it has been prewashed. If a fabric continues to bleed after two washings, consider using another fabric in your quilt.

2 For large pieces of fabric, machine wash the fabric in warm water on gentle cycle with a small amount of detergent. Be sure to group dark fabrics with dark fabrics and light with light. If the fabric piece is a yard or more, unfold it from the lengthwise way it came off the bolt, and refold it crosswise. If you have a top-loading washing machine, refolding crosswise will help prevent the fabric from twisting around the agitator.

3 Tumble dry low or spread lengthwise over a clothesline that's been covered by old towels. Do not hang wet fabric from the cut end or selvedge. Wet fabric is heavy, and this excess weight will pull it out of alignment. You can straighten fabric by pulling it in the opposite direction along its bias, which works especially well if the fabric is slightly damp.

Cut Fabric by Hand: One Template Method

In this section, you learn how to use one template to cut quilt-top squares with scissors. A good rule of thumb to remember is to use a steam iron to get all the wrinkles out of your fabric before you begin any cutting procedure.

1 Templates require a stiff material that can be used and reused such as plastic or cardboard (see Chapter 3 for suggestions). Measure, draw, and cut a 3-inch square from your template material. Be sure to use your non-fabric scissors for this task.

2 Lay the template on the wrong side of your fabric close to the selvedge. The straight edges of your square must be aligned with the lengthwise and crosswise grain of your fabric. Unless your fabric is very dark, trace around your template with a pencil. If you are marking dark fabric, you need a white or silver marking instrument. See "Other Quilting Necessities," page 29, for suggestions for markers.

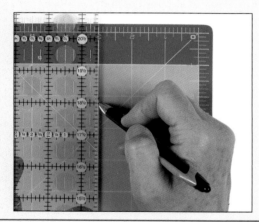

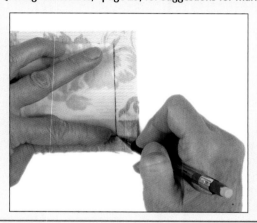

3 Before you lift up the template, be sure the pencil markings are visible.

4 Use a ruler to add ¼ inch around your drawn square for the seam allowance. Continue in this fashion until you have cut enough squares for your project.

While many quilters swear by the one-template method of cutting pieces with scissors, many others prefer using two templates. Using two templates takes much of the guesswork out of sewing because it creates an accurate seam allowance.

1 Cut two templates, one 3½ inches square, the other 3 inches square. The larger template represents the finished size of the square plus the seam allowance on all four sides.

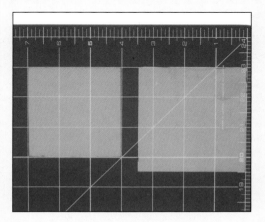

2 Lay the larger template on the wrong side of your fabric close to but not including the selvedge. Trace around it with a pencil or other marking tool. Before you lift up the template, be sure your pencil markings are visible.

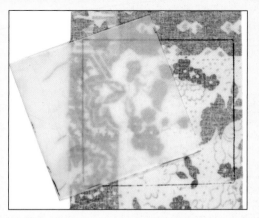

3 Center the smaller of your two templates inside the marks of the larger one that you just drew. Make sure you have a ¼-inch seam allowance on all sides of this smaller template. Check the seam allowance with your ruler. Draw around this template.

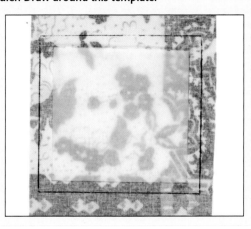

4 Cut your fabric out on the lines of the larger of the two templates. When you sew, use the interior lines as a guide for your stitching. Continue in this fashion until you have cut enough squares for your project.

Cut Fabric with a Rotary Cutter

The most important part of cutting fabric with a rotary cutter is to make certain your cuts are straight. Be as meticulous as you can because careful cutting saves you lots of headaches later. Take time to master the techniques of rotary cutting because you use them all the time if you piece your quilt tops. The process of folding, adjusting, and then cutting one edge straight is called *truing an edge*. When you work with a rotary cutter, starting with a true edge is important.

1 Fold your prewashed and ironed fabric so that its selvedges meet in a straight line with one another.

2 Lay the fabric on your cutting surface and examine the fold opposite the selvedges. It should be smooth with no wrinkles or bumps. If it is not smooth (a), slide the selvedges from side to side until the fold flattens out (b). The cut, non-selvedge edges will probably not line up with one another. That's fine. Just make certain the selvedges are aligned and the fold across from them is smooth.

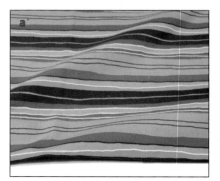

3 Bring the smoothed fold up to the selvedges so they line up perfectly with one another. Align the selvedge/fold edge (also called the *starting edge*) with one of the cutting mat's horizontal lines. Smooth and adjust the four layers of your fabric until all the parts of this starting edge—the two selvedges and the fold—meet the horizontal line perfectly. The bulk of your fabric will stretch away from your cutting hand across the mat.

④ Align the top edge of your 6 × 24-inch ruler with the top edge of your mat. Be sure these two edges are true with one another. Let the ruler lay across your fabric so there is approximately ½ inch of fabric extending beyond the right edge (left edge if you are left-handed) of your ruler. All irregularities in the fabric's edge should be clearly visible beyond your ruler's edge.

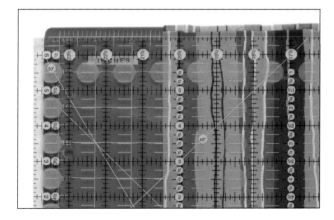

⑤ Hold the ruler firmly against your fabric with your holding hand. Take the rotary cutter in your cutting hand and place it so its silver blade hugs the side of the ruler. Start at the edge of the fabric closest to you, and use a firm, slow stroke away from your body to cut this irregular edge off your fabric. Always cut away from your body when you use a rotary cutter. Do not use short, jerky strokes when cutting.

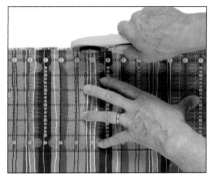

⑥ Before you raise the ruler, make sure the cut off section of fabric is completely separate from the bulk of your fabric. Sometimes a thread or two needs a second swipe of the rotary cutter before you move the ruler. If you leave more than a thread or two behind, you probably need to change your rotary cutter's blade. Do pay attention to the sharpness of your rotary cutter's blade. Cutting with a dull blade is not only frustrating, it can be dangerous.

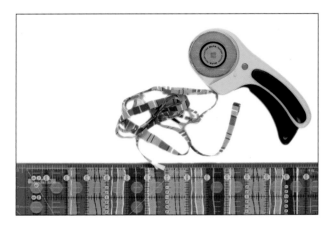

TIP

When you're cutting, it can help to let the pinky finger of your holding hand rest on your fabric to help keep the ruler from sliding.

6

Cut and Sew a Place Mat of Squares

My advice to every beginning quilter is: Start simple and start small. Face it, finishing a project is very satisfying so choose one small enough to easily start and finish. Believe me, after you tackle a few small projects, you are ready to tackle a quilt of any size.

In this chapter, you learn how to cut and sew squares together to make the top of a place mat. Even though a place mat is small, you learn every step in the quilting process. To finish this project, turn to Chapters 16 through 18 to learn how to sandwich the top with batting and a backing, quilt or tie the three layers together, and then finish it all with a binding.

Instructions for other projects made with squares start on page 76.

Math for Cutting Squares

No matter what block pattern you choose or what sort of a quilt you decide to make, understanding the math of quilting is important. Although not difficult, quilting math must be mastered in order for your finished quilt to turn out the way you want. Each of the technique chapters begins with the appropriate math and all the step-by-step calculations you need for the technique. This section explains the basic math you need to cut squares for a quilt top.

Place Mat Top Calculations

1 The finished size of these place mats is 12 × 18 inches and each square in them is 3 × 3 inches. But they did not start out that way.

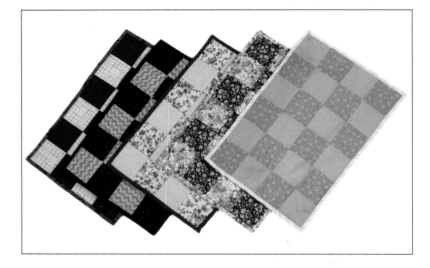

2 Unless stipulated otherwise, all quilt seam allowances are ¼ inch. A *seam allowance* is the measurement from the stitch line to the outside edge of a piece of fabric.

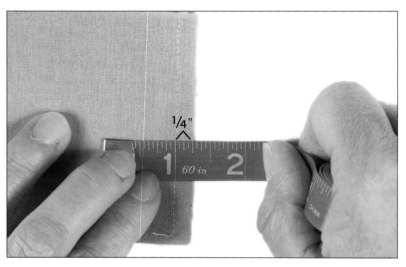

3 There is a ¼-inch seam on each of the four sides of every square in this place mat top, and these seam allowances must be included in your cutting calculations or your square's *finished size* (the way it ends up in your finished place mat) will not be accurate.

4 Here's the math for cutting a square:

Finished size of the square + ¼ inch on the left side and ¼ inch on the right side = width

¼ inch on the left + ¼ inch on the right = ½ inch total seam allowance

Finished size of the square + ¼ inch on the top and ¼ inch on the bottom = height

¼ inch on the top + ¼ inch on the bottom = ½ inch total seam allowance

The finished size of the squares in this example is 3 inches. In order to include fabric for the seam allowances, we need to cut squares measuring 3½ (width) × 3½ inches (height).

Design a Project of Squares

This project requires a total of 24 squares of fabric, each measuring 3½ × 3½ inches. The squares are sewn into four rows of six squares each. For this example, we use a simple checkerboard pattern that requires only two fabrics. For other design ideas with squares, see the project in Chapter 7.

A set of four place mats requires ½ yard of two different fabrics for the tops, ½ yard for the bindings, ¾ yard for the backings, and ¾ yard of batting.

Checkerboard Pattern

1 This checkerboard pattern depends as much on contrast as it does on color, so choose two fabrics with enough contrast to be easily differentiated from one another. For more information about contrast in fabric, see Chapter 4.

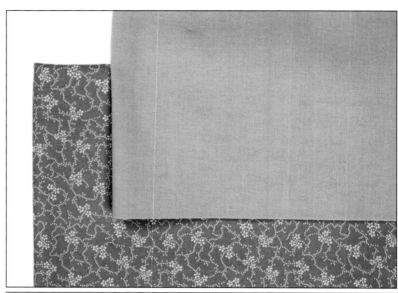

2 To cut the 12 squares of each fabric you chose for your place mat top, follow the instructions for cutting in the next section, "Rotary Cut a Place Mat Top."

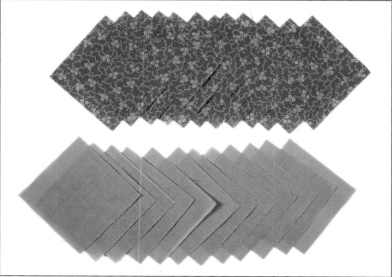

③ Once they are cut, lay your squares out on a neutral background in four rows of six squares each, alternating the fabric that begins each row.

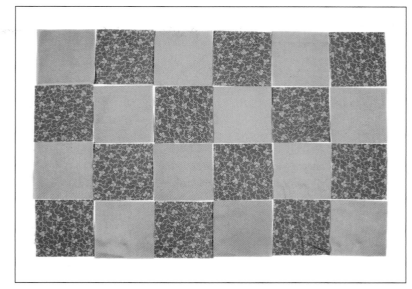

④ Once you settle on the pattern of squares, pick them up and stack them, one row at a time starting from the left and working to the right, from bottom to top. Pick up the squares in each row in the same order as the previous row. When you complete a row, slide a pin through all the squares to keep them together. Place each complete row on top of the previous one so that the whole quilt top will be in order.

TIP

Before you pick up your squares, do a quick sketch on graph paper, noting their order. Keep this paper nearby as you sew the squares together to double check yourself.

Rotary Cut a Place Mat Top

Now that you know how to true one edge of your fabric with your rotary cutter (see Chapter 5), you can cut squares for the project in this chapter. For instructions on cutting squares using scissors, please see Chapter 5.

Rotary Cut Squares

1 Place your fabric on the cutting mat with its true edge on the right, and its starting edge at the top. Align the true edge with one of the vertical inch marks on your cutting mat. Align the starting edge of your fabric (the two selvedges plus the fold) on one of the horizontal inch marks on the cutting mat. Smooth and adjust the fabric until both edges are perfectly aligned with these two perpendicular measuring lines on your mat. Make sure you can see the measurements marked on the top and bottom of your cutting mat.

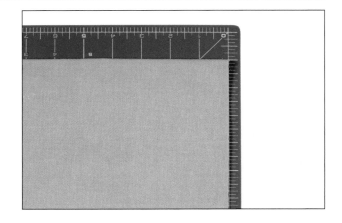

2 Start at the right edge of your fabric and measure 3½ inches to the left (a). This is the finished size of your square plus two seam allowances of ¼ inch each.

3 Align the top of your ruler with the top of the mat and place the ruler on the fabric at this 3½ inch measurement (b). Double check your measurement before you cut. Hold the ruler firmly against the fabric. Cut this strip off with your rotary cutter.

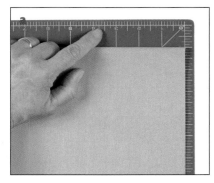

4 Before you continue, unfold this first fabric strip and take a look at it to be sure it's straight. If it bows or bends in the middle, then your selvedges are not properly aligned. Readjust your fabric, true the right edge again, cut a strip, and then examine it to be certain it's straight.

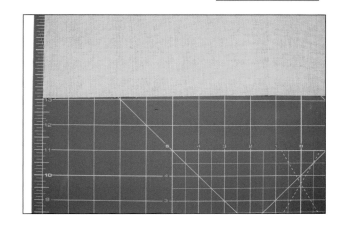

5 To finish cutting your squares, unfold a fabric strip so it's only two layers thick. Turn it 90 degrees on your cutting mat. Make sure the strip's long edge lines up with one of the vertical inch lines on your mat with the selvedge edges on the right. Place your 6 × 24-inch ruler on the fabric, making certain its top edge is accurately aligned with the top edge of your cutting mat. Place it so the selvedges extend past the right edge of your ruler. Cut off the selvedges.

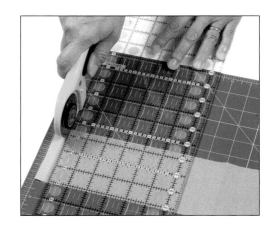

6 Now move your ruler to the left 3½ inches. Align your ruler with the top of the mat. Double check your measurement. Cut off 3½ inches of fabric. Move down the strip in 3½-inch increments, cutting off squares as you go. Be certain to keep the upper edge of the strip flush with your measuring line on the mat. Congratulations. You've just cut your first set of squares.

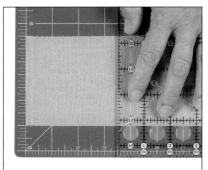

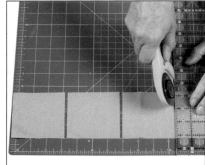

Hand Sew a Place Mat Top

Hand sewing gives a quilter a lot of control, especially when it comes to curves or the problematic junctions of several seams. Hand sewing is also very portable and involves a minimum of equipment. For those who love handwork, it can be soothing. In this section, you learn how to sew the squares for the place mat project together by hand.

Hand Sew Squares

1 Thread a needle with approximately 18 inches of thread. Do not knot it. Pick up the first two squares for the first row of your quilt top. Align their edges, right sides of the fabric facing each other. Slide a pin in at each end of the fabric, perpendicular to the direction of the seam. This prevents slipping as the pieces are sewn to one another.

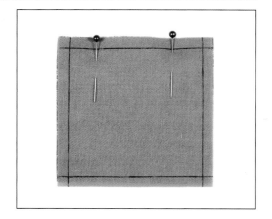

2 Start your seam with two small back stitches (a): Take one stitch forward, return to a spot next to where you began, then take a second stitch. Do not pull tight. Leave a 1 inch tail of thread.

3 Following your marked seam line, move your needle in and out of the fabric, rocking it back and forth until you have four to six stitches on the needle (b). Pull the needle through until the stitches lay flat without being tight. Finish the seam with two more back stitches.

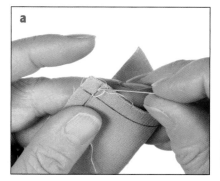

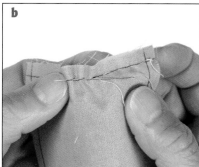

4 Sew the third square to the second, the fourth to third, and continue in this fashion until the row is complete.

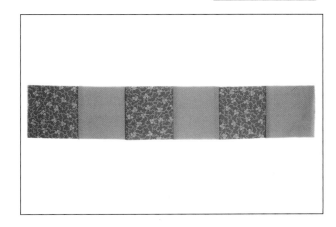

5 As you complete each new row in a quilt project, take it to the ironing board, and press both parts of each seam to one side. Press seams toward the darker of the two adjoining fabrics. This helps prevent see-through in the finished quilt top.

Note: *The difference between ironing and pressing is very important in quilting. When you iron a piece of clothing, you move the iron back and forth over the fabric's surface to get out wrinkles. In quilting, you press seams to one side. This is done with an up-and-down motion that helps prevent fabric distortion so your quilt top will lie flat.*

CONTINUED ON NEXT PAGE

TIP

Keep a squirt bottle near your ironing board to mist stubborn fabric in order to get its wrinkles out.

Sew Rows Together

1 Once the seams are pressed, align the rows, right sides facing one another. Pin them together at the seam junctions and in additional places to keep the fabric from sliding. Be very certain the seams of one row line up with the seams in the next row.

Note: *In order to keep the seams secure in a finished quilt, as you add a row, press its seam in the opposite direction of the preceding row. See page 75 later in this chapter.*

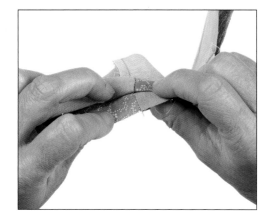

2 Join the second row to the first (a), the third to the second, and the fourth to the third (b). Always make sure you attach one row to the next in the right order. Do not pull the stitches tight. It's best to sew completed rows together once they're done so that you won't mix them up.

3 Press the row's seam to one side when you are done. If you run out of thread before a seam is complete, make two back stitches, refill your needle, and then resume sewing.

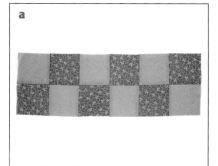

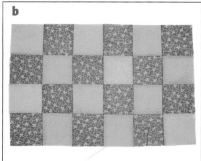

TIP

Generally speaking, the smaller the needle you use in handwork, the smaller the stitches you are able to make. For piecing a quilt, use a between needle in the size range of 10 to 12.

Sewing a quilt by machine is faster than hand sewing and the seams you make are more consistent and stronger. But machine sewing is not as portable as hand sewing and the space required to set up a machine is more than what you need for a needle and thread.

Before you begin sewing squares together, you need to be sure you are sewing a ¼-inch seam allowance. On most sewing machines, the distance from the point where the needle pushes into the fabric and the right edge of the presser foot is ¼ inch. But test this to be sure. Even a small difference can accumulate over the course of a row to make a large difference later.

① Sew two pieces of scrap together, preferably leftovers from cutting out your quilt top so that you are using the same weight fabric.

② As you sew, keep the speed of your machine slow and consistent. Slowing down allows you the time to adjust your hands on your fabric as you guide it under the needle. Pay attention to the outside edge of your seam allowance. This should be crossing the throat plate of your machine in the same place all the time. Keeping this consistent will keep your seams consistent.

③ Take the scrap off the machine, grab your tape measure, and carefully measure the seam allowance you just made. If it is not ¼ inch, make another test seam, adjusting the left-to-right placement of your fabric as you guide it under your machine's needle. Try again until you are certain you know where that line is.

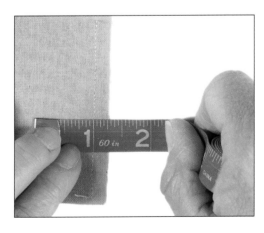

Machine Sew a Place Mat Top

Lay out Place Mat Top Pattern

1 Lay out your 24 squares in four rows of six each, keeping to your checkerboard pattern just as you started the hand-sewing process on page 67. Pick up the squares, keeping them together in rows. Be sure you pick your squares up in the same order for every row.

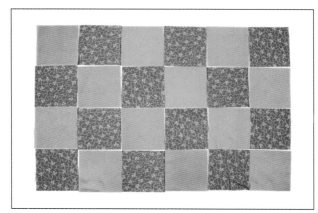

2 Take the first two squares of your first row and align them with right sides facing. Pin the two pieces together on the side you are going to stitch together to prevent the fabric from slipping as you sew.

3 Do not make any reverse stitches. Simply sew a ¼-inch seam. Clip the thread to about an inch long when you're done.

④ Continue in this fashion with the other squares in the row, double checking to make sure you're maintaining the order you set when you laid the squares out. When a row is complete, press both parts of each seam toward the darker fabric of the adjoining pieces.

⑤ Join successive rows to one another in the order you complete them, making certain the seams in each row line up exactly with one another. This precision is very important. As you add a row, press its seam in the opposite direction of the preceding row (a). This back and forth pressing helps keep the seams secure in a finished quilt project (b).

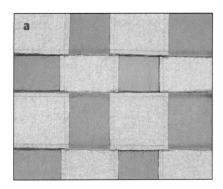
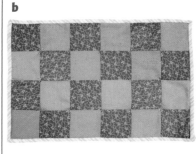

TIP

Check your graph diagram frequently as you join squares and rows to maintain the order you established for your place mat. If you join two squares or two rows in the wrong order, take the stitching out with a seam ripper, not scissors.

chapter 7

Use Squares to Construct a Baby Quilt

The simplicity of squares gives a quilter the opportunity to create all sorts of quilt-top patterns. The baby quilt featured in this chapter uses squares in four different colors to form a bold diamond rhythm that catches the eye.

Fat quarters—pieces of fabric cut to 18 × 22 inches, available in most quilting and fabric shops—can be used in this project. If you don't have a large stash yet, fat quarters provide a way to sample lots of delicious fabrics at an affordable price.

Project Overview

A quilt made of squares is simple, elegant, and gives you a wide range of design options. You can make a whole quilt of squares from just two colors, following the design instructions for the place mats in Chapter 6. You can create a quilt with strong diamond patterns, such as the one used in this project. Or play with the placement of your color selections to create your own design.

This quilt top was finished with a double border as described in Chapter 11. It is backed by a single-piece backing and filled with polyester batting as described in Chapter 16. It is hand-tied, a method described in Chapter 17 and it also is bound following instructions in Chapter 18.

WHAT YOU NEED TO KNOW

To make this quilt, you need to know how to:

> True the edge of your fabric.
> Cut a strip of a certain size using a rotary cutter, ruler, and mat.

See chapters 5 and 6 to review these skills, if necessary.

WHAT YOU WILL LEARN

In this project you will learn how to:

> Design a quilt top with multiple colors.
> Calculate the number of pieces you can cut from a piece of fabric.
> Cut multiples of the same shape at one time.
> Organize your fabric pieces before sewing a quilt top.

Materials

Yardages are given for fabrics that are 42 inches wide. If your fabric is wider or narrower, adjust these requirements accordingly.

TOP

3 fat quarters of different light fabrics plus ½ yard of a dark fabric *or*

3 pieces of different light fabrics, each ¼ of a yard plus ½ yard of dark fabric

BORDER

½ yard fabric of your choice

BACKING

1 yard

If the same fabric is chosen for the border and backing, then you can cut all the pieces from 1½ yards of fabric.

BINDING

½ yard

BATTING

1 yard. See Chapter 16 for information on batting choices.

Baby quilt in diamond pattern. Finished size: 26 × 40 inches.

Color Selection

The colors of Easter dresses and navy blue suits inspired the palette for this baby quilt. Your color scheme may harken up memories of spring flowers in bloom, the hot colors of summer, or complement a piece of your favorite fabric.

Choose Fabrics

You need four different fabrics for this quilt top: three fabrics of the same light value and one dark that will be used throughout the quilt top.

DARKS

The dark fabric squares in this quilt frame each of the light squares. You could use a solid in this quilt but a small print, such as this one, or a tone-on-tone fabric makes the top more interesting visually.

TIP

The diamond pattern of this quilt depends on contrast among its fabrics to create a stunning visual effect. Be sure to select light fabrics with strong colors so that they are not overwhelmed by your choice of dark fabric.

LIGHTS

When selecting fabrics for a quilt top, bear in mind that dark colors have a tendency to dominate the other colors around them. If your quilt top's overall pattern—the one created through the interaction of all the blocks in it—relies on strong contrast among your fabrics, you need to select light fabrics with equally strong colors.

Of the four light fabrics pictured here, the lime green will attract at least as much attention to itself as the dark fabric in the quilt top.

FABRIC SELECTION TIPS

- Bear in mind that quilt tops benefit from a certain amount of repetition. Before you select fabrics, take the time to understand how you want to use repetition in your quilt. This is best done by making sketches of your design ideas before you shop for fabrics.

- Books of quilt patterns always include examples of finished quilts. If you feel uncertain about your color selection skills—and most new quilters do—take the book with you to the fabric store to help you choose similar colors to the ones pictured.

- If you start to feel overwhelmed by the choices in a quilt shop, ask for help. Chances are good that the folks working in your local quilt shop are also quilters. Their advice can be invaluable.

How much fabric do you need to complete this quilt? Use these easy calculations to find the answer.

Calculate Yardage

1 Each finished horizontal row in this quilt consists of seven squares. Each finished square measures 3 × 3 inches.

Each finished vertical row in this quilt consists of eleven squares. In all, there are 77 squares in this quilt. There are 38 squares of navy blue, 19 of the lime green, 12 of the pink, and 8 of the pink and white. Each of your fabric pieces must be large enough to yield the appropriate number of squares.

2 You know from Chapter 6 that in order to end up with a finished 3-inch square, you need to cut a 3½-inch square (3 inches plus ¼-inch seam allowances on all four sides). Examine the two pieces of cloth in the illustration to the right. Each of them is one quarter of a yard of fabric. But the fabric on the top is a fat quarter (18 × 22 inches) and the piece on the bottom is what you get if you ask for a quarter yard of fabric (9 × 42 inches). How many 3½-inch squares can you get from each?

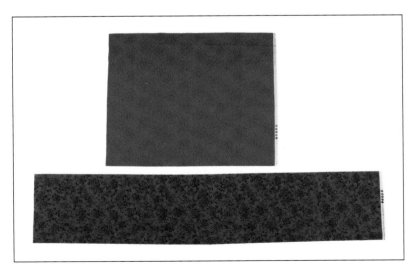

③ With any given cut of fabric, you generally lose approximately a half-inch in width and an inch in total length when you true the edge for cutting and remove the selvedges. Therefore, a 9 × 42-inch piece of fabric contains approximately 8½ × 41 inches of usable fabric for rotary cutting.

You can cut two strips measuring 3½ inches (3½ + 3½ = 7 inches) from the width of a quarter yard of fabric. Each strip yields eleven squares (11 x 3½ = 38½ inches) for a total of twenty-two squares.

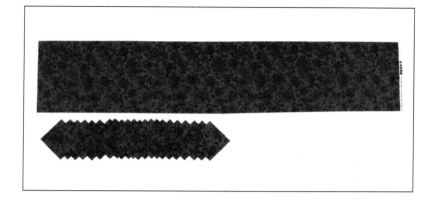

④ Because only one selvedge is removed from a fat quarter, a trimmed piece yields approximately 17½ × 21½ inches of usable fabric. First cut your 3½-inch strips perpendicular to the selvedge for a total of four strips (4 × 3½ = 14 inches). If the fat quarter is trimmed to 21½ inches, each strip yields six squares (6 × 3½ = 21½ inches). If the fat quarter is trimmed to less than 21½ inches, you get only five squares per strip (5 × 3½ = 17½ inches).

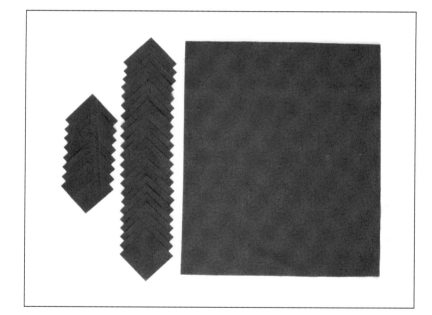

TIP

Most quilt-pattern instructions include minimum yardage requirements to complete any given project. But mistakes happen and fabric decisions change while piecing. For this reason, consider purchasing a little more fabric than the suggested minimum. If nothing else, you can add the extra fabric to your stash for a future quilt.

Cut Squares from Fat Quarters

You selected your fabrics, prewashed them (see Chapter 5), and pressed them flat. In Chapter 5, you learned how to cut squares by hand using a template. If you plan to hand cut the squares for this project with scissors, please refer to those instructions (see page 58). If you are rotary cutting your squares, here are two techniques to make this part of the process go a bit faster. If you are not cutting squares from fat quarters, please move ahead to the next section, "Cut Squares from Fabric Strips."

Cut Fat Quarters

1 These instructions explain a quick way to cut squares from two fat quarters at one time. Position your cutting mat so that its longest dimension is horizontal on your worktable. Layer the fat quarters on your cutting mat so that their selvedges are aligned with each other and with the measuring line at the top of your mat. True the edge of your fabrics following the instructions in Chapter 5, removing the least amount of fabric possible.

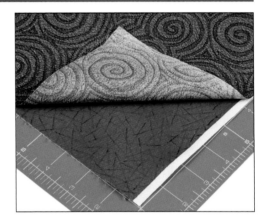

2 Rotate your mat 90 degrees or reposition your body so that the longest dimension of the mat is vertical on your worktable (a). Lay down your ruler and cut off the selvedges, removing as little fabric as possible. Reposition your fabric so that the two trimmed edges are aligned with the vertical and horizontal 1-inch lines on your mat.

3 Return your mat to its original position (b). Working from right to left, measure 3½ inches and cut your first strips.

④ Turn your mat 90 degrees. Make sure the sets of strips are aligned vertically and horizontally with measurements on the mat. Working from right to left, measure 3½ inches and cut your first set of squares.

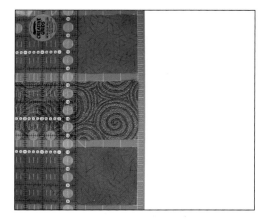

⑤ Continue in this fashion until all the squares are cut from your fat quarters.

For most quilt projects, it makes sense to sort your squares into their respective colors once you are done cutting. This makes the squares easier to manipulate as you lay out your quilt top for sewing.

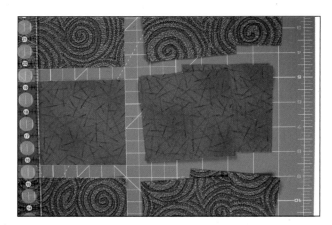

TIP

You should stop halfway through your cut, carefully leave the rotary cutter in place, reposition your left hand higher up on your ruler, and then finish your cut. This step helps prevent the ruler from slipping.

Remember—before you cut, always double-check your fabric's alignment.

Cut Squares from Fabric Strips

If you are not using fat quarters for this project, begin cutting the squares for this quilt by cutting strips following the directions in Chapter 6 (see page 68). This section starts with a quick review followed by a way to cut multiple squares at once.

Cut Strips

1 Align your selvedges and fold your fabric for cutting by following the instructions in Chapter 6. Even the edge of your fabric.

2 Once you have evened your edge, realign your fabric with a horizontal measuring mark on your mat. Being careful not to disturb the fabric's placement, move your ruler 3½ inches to the left (a) and cut a strip. Move your ruler 3½ inches again and cut a second strip in the same fashion.

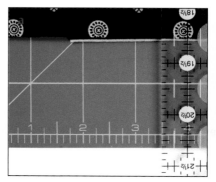
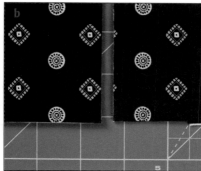

3 Keep your strips of fabric doubled, and lay them on your cutting mat with the selvedge ends on the same side as your cutting hand. You can fit five strips of this size at a time on your cutting mat. Align each strip with a horizontal measuring line. Lay your ruler down and cut off the selvedge edges.

4 Working toward your non-cutting hand, measure 3½ inches and cut across all five strips with one stroke. Stop cutting about halfway through your stroke (don't move the rotary cutter), and move your left hand higher up on your ruler to keep it from sliding.

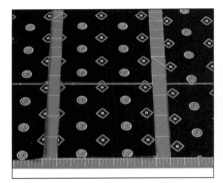

5 Your fabric strips should *always* line up with the horizontal marks on the cutting mat, so you will have squares of the same size. Continue cutting off squares at 3½-inch increments.

6 After cutting four or five sets of squares, realign your strips as shown, and then resume cutting.

When you have cut all your squares, put all of the same color squares together in a pile.

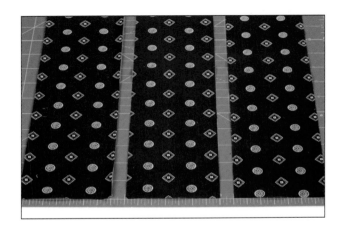

Design the Quilt Top

Now that your squares are cut, arrange them in a pleasing design. Choose an open area of your workspace or home for this fun process, a place big enough to arrange and rearrange your squares. The following steps will guide you in arranging your squares so that the colors form a diamond pattern in the finished quilt top.

① Cover your design space with a neutral color (white, cream, or gray) or choose a floor space of a neutral color, somewhere that your fabric will not be disturbed as you lay it out. In this quilt top, the dark fabrics function as a grid so they are laid out with spaces between them to accommodate the light fabric squares.

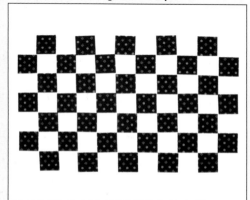

② Choose squares of the strongest color among your light fabrics. In order to accentuate their impact, place one in the center of the quilt and one in each corner.

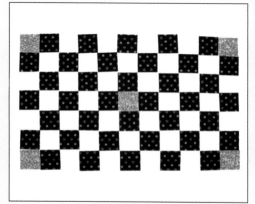

③ Add more squares of your strongest light color among the dark squares in a diamond configuration. Refer to the photograph below for guidance.

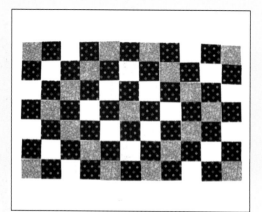

④ Of the remaining light colors, the white squares with the pink design are the next strongest. Following the diamond pattern established in the previous step, add your next strongest light fabric squares to your layout as pictured.

5 There are two light colored fabrics left of the four we started with, a pink and a lavender. Which one works best in this quilt top? If you are undecided between two (or more) fabrics or colors, it's helpful to lay some of each in your quilt top to measure their impact.

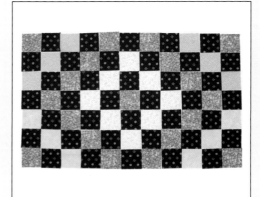

6 In order to keep the bright spring color theme of this quilt top intact, the pink is the better choice. Once you have laid out your quilt top in this way, stand back from it. Make any adjustments in color or arrangement until you are satisfied.

7 Once you have laid out all your rows, make a quick sketch of your design or take a digital picture of it to use as a reference when it comes time to sew the quilt together.

8 Here's how to gather squares for sewing. Starting with the block on the left, as you take up each row, place each successive block below the one in your hand. When you have a whole row, pin its blocks together with a piece of paper on which the row number is marked. Lay your rows out in numerical order. This is the order in which they will be sewn.

Piece the Quilt Top

After all the cutting and stacking is done, now put your quilt top together. Gather your fabric squares and head for the sewing machine.

Join Rows

1. Starting with the first and second squares of your first row, pin the squares with right sides facing, and sew together with a ¼-inch seam. Sew the third square in the row to the second, the fourth to the third, and so on across the row. When completed, press both sides of each seam toward the darker fabrics.

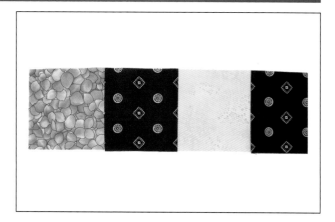

TIP

If you sew a square in the wrong order, remove the stitching with a seam ripper, press the squares flat, and re-sew. Also, when machine sewing one row to another, stop sewing just before a seam between squares is about to move under the presser foot of your machine. With the needle in the fabric, raise the presser foot just a little in order to let the fabric of the seam lie flat. Wait until the machine's needle has caught the fabric of a seam before taking out the pin holding it. This will help keep your seams lined up. Sliding the pin under the fabric while the machine is stopped helps to make sure that seams on the underside of the work are lying flat as well.

It is not a good idea to machine stitch over pins in fabric. If the needle on your machine hits a pin, it can break. Even if your machine's needle doesn't break, you should change it if you hit a pin because the needle's tip will be blunted or the needle may be bent.

2 Sew your second row of squares together, making sure you attach them to one another in the right order. Press both sides of the seams toward the darker fabrics.

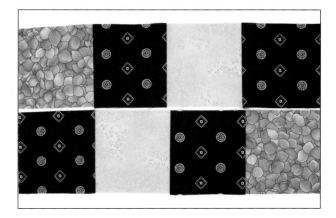

3 Sew rows together as you complete them so that their order will not become confused. The seams joining the squares should line up with one another when you put the rows together. Use your fingers to slide the fabric of two rows from side to side with little movements until you feel the seams slide into place with one another. If the seams are pressed in opposite directions from one another, you can almost feel them *lock* into place when they are correctly aligned.

4 Press both sides of each row's seam to one side. Alternate the direction of this pressing with each successive row. This alternate pressing helps lock in the seams to make the overall quilt top stronger than if all the seams were pressed in the same direction.

Finish your quilt project by following the instructions in chapters 16 through 18. See Chapter 11 for instructions on adding a border.

Work with Rectangles: Broken Bricks Pattern

From squares, we go to rectangles. The rectangle shape is used all by itself in patterns such as the Broken Bricks featured in this chapter or in combination with other shapes, as you will see in upcoming chapters. The rectangle also is used in blocks such as the Log Cabin pattern (see Chapter 10).

Broken Bricks is a carefree and simple pattern, perfect for experimenting with color. This quilt features blues and reds but it could be done in various values of the same color (*monochromatic*) or in any of the other color combinations suggested in Chapter 4. The quilt's size, 42" x 54" makes it perfect for using fat quarters, too.

Broken Bricks
Pattern Overview

Traditionally, the Broken Bricks pattern features rectangles of the same size mixed with rectangles that are half the size of the original, each size appearing in a regular rhythm throughout the quilt.

For this quilt, I alternate the two color families (red, blue, red, blue) in each row, but mix the two sizes of rectangles at random. The result is a playful quilt that yields some surprising color combinations.

This quilt top is finished with a double border (see Chapter 11), backed by a one-piece backing, and filled with polyester batting (see Chapter 16). The hand-tying method used in this quilt is described in Chapter 17, and the binding in Chapter 18.

WHAT YOU NEED TO KNOW

For this project, you need to know:

How to true the edge of a piece of fabric, and how to cut strips to a certain size using a rotary cutter, ruler, and mat. (See chapters 5 and 6.)

Cut multiples of the same shape at a time. (See Chapter 7.)

Design a quilt top before sewing. (See Chapter 7.)

WHAT YOU WILL LEARN

In this project, you will learn how to:

Combine fabric shapes of different sizes in a quilt top.

Calculate the dimensions of fabric shapes of different sizes.

Materials

Yardages are given for fabrics that are 42 inches wide. If your fabric is wider or narrower, you need to adjust these requirements accordingly. Fat quarters should measure no less than 18 × 22 inches.

TOP

11 fat quarters, 6 of blue, 5 of red (or equivalent in your chosen colors) *or*

11 pieces of fabric, each ¼ of a yard

BORDER (CUT CROSSWISE)

¾ yard of a neutral (a muslin colored fabric) that does not appear in the quilt top

¾ yard of a blue that appears in the quilt (or one of the color families in your fabrics)

BACKING

1½ yards

If the same fabric is chosen for one of the borders and backing, then you can cut all the pieces from 2 yards of fabric.

BINDING

½ yard

BATTING

One crib-sized batt, 45 × 60 inches. See Chapter 16 for information on batting choices.

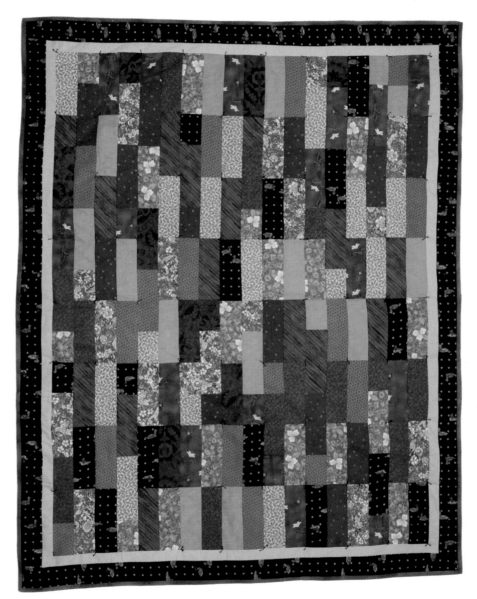

Broken Bricks pattern quilt. Finished size: 42 × 54 inches.

Measure and Cut Quilt Top Pieces

No matter what shape you're cutting for a quilt, always include the ¼-inch seam allowance in your calculations. You got a feel for this when you calculated the correct size for the squares in the quilt projects in chapters 6 and 7. In this chapter, you will learn how to take seam allowances into account when calculating the measurements of pieces that are not the same size.

Cut Full Bricks

1 The finished size of the full-sized rectangles (I refer to them as bricks for this project) in this quilt is 2 × 6 inches. Using the same method you learned for squares in Chapter 6, add ½ inch (the equivalent of two ¼-inch seams) to both the length and width of the finished size in order to calculate the proper size to cut for the rectangle pieces. For this quilt top, cut bricks that are 2½ × 6½ inches.

Note: Keep all of the bricks of each fabric together once the pieces are cut. If you are using fat quarters, save the leftover fabric from each strip for your half bricks.

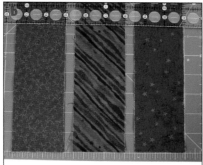

2 You need 12 full-sized bricks like the ones pictured above (a) from each of your 11 fabrics. For fat quarters, one strip (2½ × 18 inches) yields 2 full-sized bricks, so cut a total of six strips from each fat quarter. For yardage, one strip (2½ × 42 inches) yields 6 full-sized bricks so cut two strips.

3 Lay your 2½-inch strips on your cutting mat (b) and cut pieces 6½ inches long. You now have a total of 132 rectangles measuring 2½ × 6½ inches.

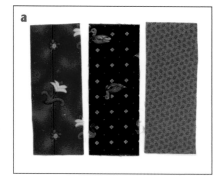

Cut Half Bricks

1 If you've ever looked closely at bricks in a wall, you know they usually are not stacked directly on top of one another. The bricks are offset so that the mortar seams are not aligned with one another, which strengthens the wall. The Broken Bricks quilt pattern imitates this concept by scattering half-sized bricks among the full-sized ones.

2 The finished size of the half bricks in this quilt top is 2×3 inches. It would seem logical that you could just take one of the full-sized bricks, cut it in half, and include it in the quilt top, doesn't it? But if you did, you would cut pieces measuring $2\frac{1}{2} \times 3\frac{1}{4}$ inches. If you used half bricks of this unfinished size, their finished size would end up $2\frac{1}{2} \times 2\frac{3}{4}$ inches (to account for seam allowances). In order to achieve a finished size of 2×3 inches, you need half bricks cut to $2\frac{1}{2} \times 3\frac{1}{2}$ inches.

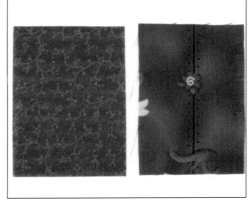

3 There are 36 half-sized bricks scattered throughout this quilt top. If you cut your full-sized bricks from fat quarters, use the leftovers to cut bricks measuring $2\frac{1}{2} \times 3\frac{1}{2}$ inches. Scatter your cutting among your fabrics, taking an average of 4 half-bricks from each fabric.

Organize and Piece Your Quilt Top

Now that the cutting is complete, you can sew your quilt top together. But before you start sewing, take the time to organize your bricks for your quilt top.

---

1 Think of your cut fabric pieces as paints on a palette. Visual artists keep their colors organized so that they can go back and forth between their paints and canvas with ease. Before you begin sewing, take some time to organize your own palette by putting all the pieces of the same fabric in the same pile, with full and half bricks separated. No matter what block pattern you use, always remember that a little organization before you begin to sew saves you lots of headaches later on.

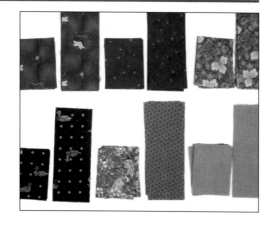

2 Examine this detail of the Broken Bricks pattern carefully. Note that the rows contain various combinations of full- and half-sized bricks. Every full row in this top is either 8 full-sized bricks or their equivalent. Some rows contain 7 full-sized bricks and 2 half bricks. Others contain 6 full-sized bricks and 4 half-sized ones. In order for all the rows to end up the same length, each row must be one of these three combinations.

③ Before you begin to sew, lay out your pieces in rows as you did for the projects made of squares in chapters 6 and 7. Once your rows are established and you are satisfied with the way they look together, pick your fabric pieces up as you did with the squares, taking care to order your bricks the same way for each row. Note that the half bricks are scattered among the rows one by one instead of in pairs. This scattering ensures that the seams between the bricks are offset from one another when the rows are sewn together.

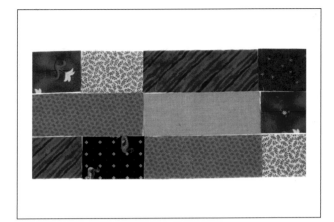

④ Join your bricks to one another as you did the squares in chapters 6 and 7. Press both sides of the seams toward the darker fabric. Join the rows to one another as you complete them. Note that some seams between the bricks line up with one another when you join the rows and some do not. When two brick seams coincide, be sure to align them as you did in the squares project in Chapter 7.

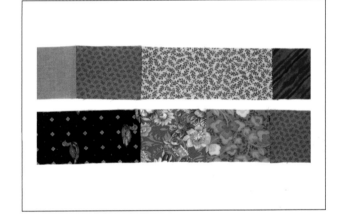

TIP

As you pin rows together, give your fabric a little stretch to make sure it's flat. Over the course of pinning a long row, these little stretches accumulate so that when you get to the end of your pinning, one row is a bit longer than the other, even though they started out the same size. This discrepancy can be alleviated if you pin from the ends to the middle.

Put the two left edges together at their corners, slide in a pin, and then move to the two right edges, align them and pin them. Then move back to the left, back to the right, and so on until you've pinned the two rows together.

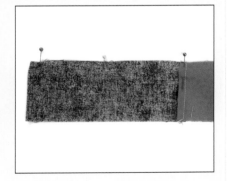

chapter

9

Introduction to Strip Sets: Fence Rail Pattern

When quilters discovered the rotary cutter, piecing a quilt top was never the same. Hundreds of traditional patterns as well as new ones make use of what quilters call *strip sets* that were made possible by the rotary cutter. A strip set consists of two or more strips of fabric sewn together and then cut to create new design elements to be incorporated into quilt tops. If a quilter cuts several strips at a time, this process is often referred to as *stripping.*

Fence Rail is one of the oldest-known quilt patterns. Without the rotary cutter, the three pieces in each block are cut individually by hand using a template, and then sewn together one at a time. The strip piecing techniques shown in this chapter simplify that process.

Fence Rail Pattern Overview

The number of individual strips in a Fence Rail block varies from two to seven. Fabrics for a Fence Rail block are chosen for their contrast, as in this project, or because they are variations of the same hue.

The zigzag pattern in this quilt top is achieved by alternating the direction of the individual Fence Rail blocks so that the lightest and darkest fabrics abut one another. When the quilt top is complete, the outlines of the individual blocks disappear because they are "absorbed" into the top's overall pattern.

This quilt top is finished with a narrow single border (see Chapter 11). It is backed by a three-piece backing and filled with polyester batting as described in Chapter 16. It is hand tied, a method described in Chapter 17, and the binding is described in Chapter 18.

WHAT YOU NEED TO KNOW

For this project, you need to know how to:

> True the edge of a piece of fabric and cut strips to a certain size using a rotary cutter, ruler, and mat. (See chapters 5 and 6.)
>
> Cut multiples of the same shape at a time and design a quilt top before sewing. (See Chapter 7.)

WHAT YOU WILL LEARN

In this project, you will learn how to:

> Combine strips of different fabrics into one block.
> Create an overall quilt-top pattern that takes advantage of the contrast between dark and light fabrics.

Materials

Yardages are given for fabrics that are 42 inches wide. If your fabric is wider or narrower, you need to adjust these requirements accordingly.

TOP

You can use one or two midtones in this project.

If you use one midtone: ½ yard each of a light fabric, a dark, and a midtone

If you use two midtones: ½ yard dark fabric; ½ yard light fabric; ¼ yard of each midtone.

BORDER (CUT CROSSWISE)

½ yard of dark fabric or other fabric of your choice

BACKING

1½ yards

BINDING

½ yard

BATTING

One crib-sized batt, 45 × 60 inches. See Chapter 16 for information on batting choices.

Fence Rail quilt. Finished size 42 × 54 inches.

Contrast between fabrics is crucial for the success of this version of the Fence Rail block. This is a great pattern to help you understand the true value of dark and light in quilting.

Contrast is Key

1 This Fence Rail pattern's success depends entirely on the contrast between the darkest and lightest fabrics (a). The midtones work best if they are subtle in color. This pattern benefits from repetition so stick to the same three (or four, if you use two midtones) fabrics throughout.

2 You can use a monochromatic color scheme (b). But take care to choose a very dark and a very light value of your chosen color or the Fence Rail's zigzag pattern will not be evident.

3 This color selection for a Fence Rail is fine if the block is meant to blend in with another block pattern. But it is not a good choice for this project. Before you settle on final fabric choices, make a sample block, pin it up on a wall, walk about 10 feet away, and then look at the block. Can you immediately see the difference between the dark and light fabrics? If yes, they are good choices.

Calculations for the Fence Rail block include two considerations: the finished size of the completed block and the size of the individual strips in it.

Calculations

1 The finished size of an individual block in this quilt top is 6 × 6 inches. Therefore, the finished width of each strip is 2 inches. To calculate the unfinished size of each strip, add in the seam allowances on all four sides.

2 When you add your ¼-inch seam allowance to the length of each individual strip, you get an unfinished length of 6½ inches (6 + ¼ + ¼). When you add a ¼-inch seam allowance to the width of each strip, you get an unfinished width of 2½ inches (2 + ¼ + ¼).

3 When you add these two dimensions together, you need three strips of fabric measuring 2½ × 6½ inches per Fence Rail block. If you cut each of these pieces by hand, it is tedious. But strip sets make this whole process easier.

Cut and Sew Strip Sets

Once you learn the basics of strip sets in this chapter, you discover an amazing array of ways to use them in quilting. Strip sets serve as the basic design elements in a wide variety of quilts. They are cut, sewed together, recut and resewed to create all sorts of lovely patterns of color and shape.

Cut Out Strips and Pin Together

1 Prewash and iron your fabrics before you cut your strips. Following the instructions in Chapter 5, true the right edge of your folded fabric. If you are using only one midtone, cut 11 strips measuring 2½ inches wide from each fabric. If you are using two midtones, cut 11 strips measuring 2½ inches wide from the dark and light fabrics along with 6 strips from each of the midtones.

Note: If your cutting table is shorter than your fabric, carefully fold up the trailing end of fabric while you cut (see photo). This step relieves the weight of the yardage so the fabric won't pull away from your ruler and rotary cutter as you slice off your strips.

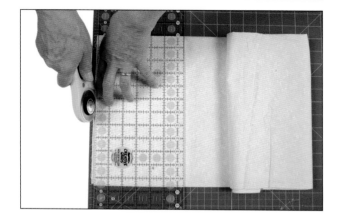

2 With right sides facing one another, pin a strip of light to a strip of midtone fabric (a); sew them together, then press both sides of the seam toward the midtone fabric.

3 Take care not to stretch the fabric as you pin, but don't be surprised if the strips are not exactly the same size. Fabric off the bolt often varies in width. Your light fabric may be 41¾ inches wide while your midtone is only 41 inches (b). For now, leave the difference in place.

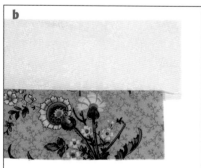

Sew Strip Sets Together

1 Strip sets are always sewed together in the same order throughout a quilt top's construction. In this Fence Rail pattern, for example, the midtone fabric always separates the light and dark fabrics. When creating these Fence Rail strip sets, never sew the light and dark fabrics to one another.

2 To complete this strip set, sew the dark fabric to the midtone fabric. Press both sides of the seam toward the dark fabric. For this project, complete 11 strip sets.

TIP

While quilting, do the same parts of a project in the same way. In these strip sets, for example, make a habit of joining the midtone and light fabrics first, then sew the dark to the midtone fabric. As you will see in the Log Cabin blocks in Chapter 10, the order of sewing really makes a difference.

Cut Strip Sets into Blocks

In practice, a strip set is a large design element that yields small design elements. In other words, what you have sewed together, you are now going to cut apart.

Cut 66 Fence Rail Blocks

1 Remember those uneven edges referred to in the previous section? Now you cut them off. Use the same method to true the right edge of a strip set that you use to true the edge of fabric before you cut strips.

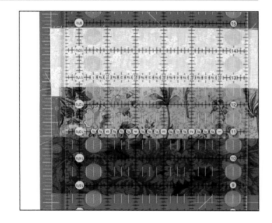

2 Align the top and right edges of a strip set on your cutting mat, place your ruler at 6½ inches (the unfinished size of a Fence Rail block), and cut. Continue in this fashion through all 11 strip sets, cutting six blocks from each one. You will end up with 66 Fence Rail blocks in all. If you included two different midtone fabrics, divide your Fence Rail blocks into two piles according to those fabrics.

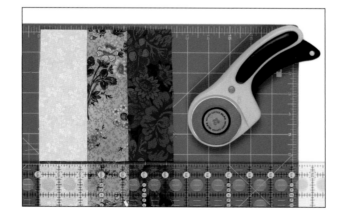

It is wonderful to think that nothing ever goes wrong when you make a quilt. But that's simply not true. Fabric, however, is pretty forgiving. From time to time, I suggest ways to fix an oops in your quilting.

Re-true the Edge

1 As you cut your blocks, you may notice that the upper edge of your strip set curves slightly away from a straight line (a). Over the course of pinning and sewing long strips, fabric can be stretched with your fingers as you pin or by the pull of the feed dogs on a sewing machine.

2 If your top edge curves away from straight, adjust the top of your strip set until you have aligned as much of this edge as possible with a horizontal measuring line on your mat (b).

 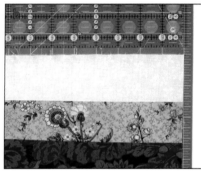

3 When you align your top edge, your right edge veers away from straight. Lay down your ruler and re-true the right edge just as you would true the edge of any fabric. The fabric you remove during this procedure is minimal, and truing the edge may need to be done more than once as you move along a strip set.

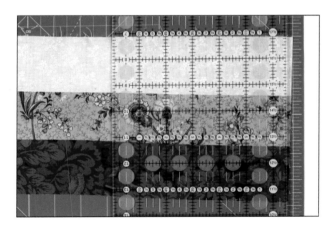

Once the Fence Rail blocks are cut, sewing the quilt top together goes quickly, and it's fun to watch the zigzag pattern emerge as you join the rows together.

Piece Together Fence Rail Blocks

1 If you include two different midtone fabrics in your Fence Rail blocks, separate them into two piles according to the fabric. As you join blocks to one another, alternate these blocks. For example, the quilt pictured at the beginning of this chapter alternates the green and pink midtones as you move across a row. If you use the same three fabrics in all your Fence Rail blocks, simply pile the blocks next to your sewing machine or next to you as you hand sew.

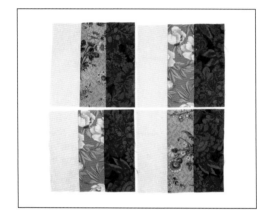

2 There's a rhythm to the way the blocks connect to one another. The first row block pattern is: light fabric on left, light fabric on top, repeating across the first row.

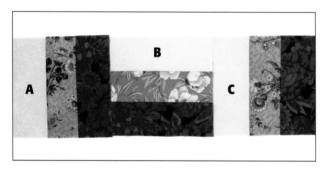

3 The second row block pattern is: light fabric strip on top, light fabric strip on left, repeating across the second row. These two row patterns repeat one after the other through all nine rows in the quilt top.

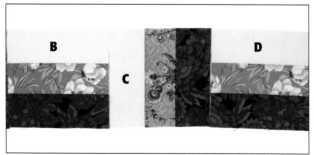

④ I recommend joining rows to one another as you complete them so their order is not confused. But before you sew on a new row, take the time to lay it out next to your growing quilt top to be certain you attach it the right way. A few moments of checking first can save you lots of time with a seam ripper later.

⑤ Carefully pin your rows of Fence Rail blocks together so that the seams between blocks are accurately aligned with one another. The overall zigzag of a Fence Rail quilt depends on the visual flow of one block into another. If seams are misaligned, it jars the eye.

⑥ As you join one row to the next, the distinctive zigzag pattern of the Fence Rail quilt emerges as if by magic. When it's all together, the individual blocks of the Fence Rail disappear into the overall quilt pattern.

chapter 10

Variation in Strip Sets: Log Cabin Pattern

The first Log Cabin block pattern appeared in the United States in the mid-1800s and has been a favorite with quilters ever since. While no one's quite sure how many different variations there are of Log Cabin, one collector I know has catalogued more than 150 different block patterns. Traditionally, the Log Cabin block starts with a square of red fabric in the center to represent the glowing hearth of a nineteenth-century home. As additional strips of cloth are added, half of them are light fabrics, half dark. See Chapter 15 for instructions.

I selected a variation of the Log Cabin for this chapter that relies on strip sets so you can build on the strip set lessons in Chapter 9.

Log Cabin Pattern Overview

While all quilt block patterns play with color and contrast, no pattern emphasizes these important concepts like the Log Cabin. The geometric structure of this block requires close attention to cutting and sewing.

If you're a beginning quilter, study the block-pattern variations included in the "Experiment with Various Designs" section, later in this chapter. You can make a pillow top with as few as four Log Cabin blocks, or a star wall hanging with 16 blocks. In order to practice your skills, try your hand at one of these small projects before moving on to a quilt for a queen-sized bed.

These two Log Cabin quilts (opposire page) are finished without border, backed by one-piece backings, and filled with polyester batting as described in Chapter 16. They are hand tied, a method described in Chapter 17, and their bindings are described in Chapter 18.

The wall hanging on this page is the Star 2 pattern on page 124 of this chapter.

WHAT YOU NEED TO KNOW

For this project, you need to know:

How to true the edge of a piece of fabric and cut strips to a certain size using a rotary cutter. (See chapters 5 and 6.)
How to create a strip set. (See Chapter 9.)

WHAT YOU WILL LEARN

In this project, you will learn how to:

Analyze a block pattern in order to understand its design elements.
Create a block pattern by combining a variety of strip sets.

Materials

Please note, these fabric requirements cover what you need to make the 16 Log Cabin blocks featured in the wall hanging on this page. The left quilt on the opposite page (36 × 45 inches) requires 48 blocks so adjust your yardage accordingly.

TOP

¾ yard total of various dark fabrics

¾ yard total of various light fabrics

Please note, 8 different light fabrics and 8 different dark fabrics are used in this quilt top. Quilters use the term *scrappy* to refer to quilt tops made from a wide variety of fabrics. Choose fabrics with a lot of contrast to one another in terms of dark and light. This is not a block pattern for midtones.

BACKING

½ yard of fabric that appears in quilt top or other cotton fabric of your choice

BINDING

¼ yard of fabric that appears in quilt top or other fabric of your choice

BATTING

One crib-sized batt, 45 × 60 inches. See Chapter 16 for information on batting choices.

Log Cabin variations. Finished size: 36 × 45 inches (left), 24 × 24 inches (right).

Log Cabin Block Analysis and Quilting Math

Generally speaking, quilters have two reactions when they see a quilt for the first time: They admire the color selections from afar and then they draw closer to see how the top is put together. Or as a quilting friend of mine puts it: "What's the block?"

To understand how the block is put together, I break this Log Cabin pattern down into the individual components.

Analyze a Block

1. Like the Fence Rail blocks in Chapter 9, Log Cabin blocks should blend together to create an overall pattern in a quilt top. Once they are sewn to one another, it's difficult to see where one block ends and the next begins.

2. The first step in quilt pattern analysis is to find the individual blocks in a finished quilt. You do this by locating the joining seams between blocks and between rows so that you can isolate an individual block (a).

3. When seen apart, it's easier to understand how the blocks work with one another (b). But what about the individual logs in each block?

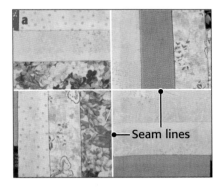

Seam lines

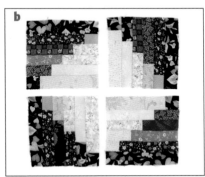

Quilt Math

1 The finished size of one Log Cabin block is 6 × 6 inches. Because there are six logs in each block, the finished width of each log is 1 inch. Note that each log is made up of two pieces of fabric of varying lengths.

2 When you add seam allowances to the length of a finished block, you get an unfinished size of 6½ inches. When you add seam allowances to the width of each log, you get an unfinished size of 1½ inches.

3 As you view one of these Log Cabin blocks from left to right, notice that the ratio of dark fabric to light changes in increments of 1 inch per log. But while the dark/light ratio changes, the unfinished size of each two-piece log always equals the unfinished size of the single-piece log: 6½ inches. So how do you figure out how big each individual piece is?

CONTINUED ON NEXT PAGE

4 Each part of this two-piece log pictured here has four seam allowances: ¼ inch on each side (1 inch + ¼ inch + ¼ inch = 1½ width) and ¼ inch on each end. In the finished quilt, the length of the dark fabric in this picture is 4 inches. When you add seam allowances to it, the unfinished size becomes 4½ inches (4 + ¼ + ¼). The finished length of the light fabric is 2 inches. When you add its seam allowances, the unfinished length becomes 2½ inches.

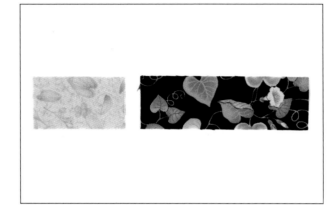

5 Keeping those seam allowances in mind, the breakdown of lengths of the pieces in each individual log follows. Remember, every piece is 1½ inches wide.

Log 1 – 6½ inches of dark fabric

Log 2 – 5½ inches of dark fabric, 1½ inches of light fabric

Log 3 – 4½ inches of dark fabric, 2½ inches of light fabric

Log 4 – 3½ inches of dark fabric, 3½ inches of light fabric

Log 5 – 2½ inches of dark fabric, 4½ inches of light fabric

Log 6 – 1½ inches of dark fabric, 5½ inches of light fabric

If all this quilting math seems confusing, don't worry. I translate it here into directions for strip sets. This set of instructions yields enough logs for 16 Log Cabin blocks. Increase or decrease the number of logs you cut for the pattern of your choice. Use a variety of dark and light fabrics for your strip sets.

Log 1: True the edge of one dark fabric. Cut a strip 6½ in. wide. Turn the strip and cut 16 logs 1½ in. wide.

Log 2: True the edge of one dark and one light fabric. Cut a dark strip 5½ in. wide. Cut a light strip 1½ in. wide. Sew the two strips together, press the seam toward the dark fabric. Cut 16 logs 1½ in. wide.

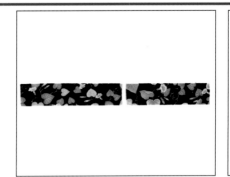
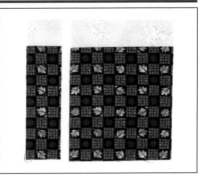

Log 3: True the edge of one dark and one light fabric. Cut a dark strip 4½ in. wide and light strip 2½ in. wide. Sew strips together, press seam toward dark fabric. Cut 16 logs 1½ in. wide.

Log 4: True the edge of one dark and one light fabric. Cut dark strip 3½ in. wide and light strip 3½ in. wide. Sew strips together, press seam toward dark fabric. Cut 16 logs 1½ in. wide.

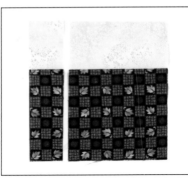

Log 5: True the edge of one dark and one light fabric. Cut dark strip 2½ in. wide and light strip 4½ in. wide. Sew strips together, press seam toward dark fabric. Cut 16 logs 1½ in. wide.

Log 6: True the edge of one dark and one light fabric. Cut a dark strip 1½ in. wide and a light strip 5½ in. wide. Sew strips together, press seam toward dark fabric. Cut 16 logs 1½ in. wide.

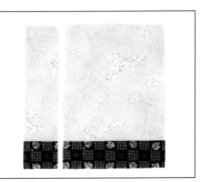

Combine Strip Set Logs into a Block

When you create a quilt block out of separate pieces, organize your pieces and your process of joining them to one another in such a way that all the finished blocks turn out the same. This is especially necessary in this Log Cabin pattern, where you must sew each block together in the same order so that the contrasting colors are organized the same way in every block.

Organize and Sew

1 Once all your logs are cut, organize them so that all the logs with the same color ratios are together. Line them up from the single piece of dark fabric to the log that's mostly light fabric. This is the order in which you will attach them to one another.

Note: Take your time putting the logs together and handle the blocks with care. When you sew lots of small pieces together, the overall block becomes stretchy. Also, see the section on pressing at the end of this chapter for specifics that apply to Log Cabin blocks.

2 Always start with the single log of dark fabric. Hold it so that its right side is facing you. Pick up log 2 and pin the logs to one another with the light fabric on the left side (a).

3 One more item of importance as you sew these logs together—when you pin a new log to the preceding logs, make sure that the new log's wrong side is facing you (b). If you use the habits in steps 2 and 3, all of your Log Cabin blocks should turn out fine.

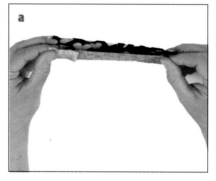

a

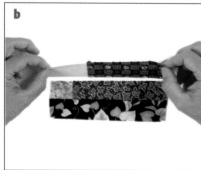

b

With a minimum of 16 blocks of this Log Cabin variation you can make at least 14 different quilt-top patterns. Two pictures for each pattern are shown over the next few pages. The first picture shows the blocks apart from one another so you can see how they are joined to the others. The blocks in the second picture are close to one another so the pattern is clearer.

DARK WITH LIGHT

Dark with light square—blocks apart (left).

Dark with light square—blocks together (right).

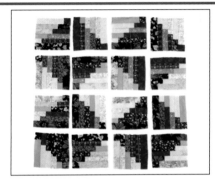 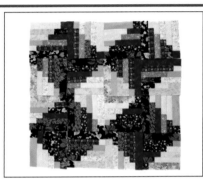

LIGHT WITH DARK

Light with dark square—blocks apart (left).

Light with dark square—blocks together (right).

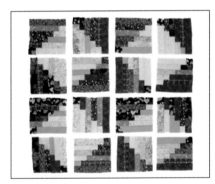 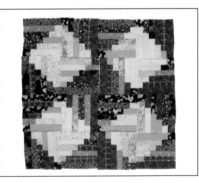

BIRDS IN FLIGHT

Birds in Flight pattern—blocks apart (left).

Birds in Flight pattern—blocks together (right).

CONTINUED ON NEXT PAGE

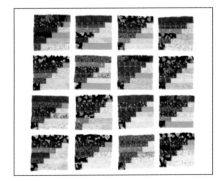 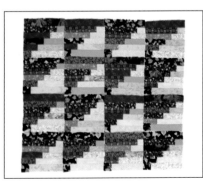

ZIGZAG

Zigzag pattern—blocks apart (left).

Zigzag pattern—blocks together (right).

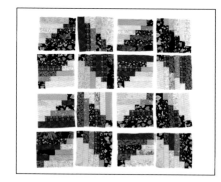

ARROW

Arrow pattern—blocks apart (left).

Arrow pattern—blocks together (right).

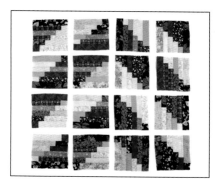
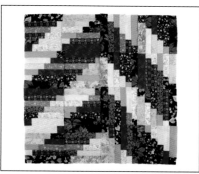

COMING AND GOING

Coming and Going pattern—blocks apart (left).

Coming and Going pattern—blocks together (right).

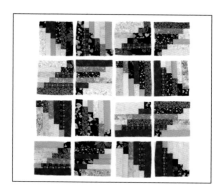
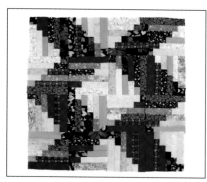

FIELDS AND FURROWS

Fields and Furrows pattern—blocks apart (left).

Fields and Furrows pattern—blocks together (right).

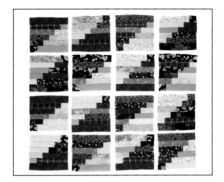
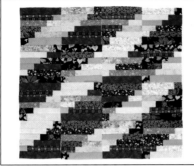

BARN RAISING

Barn Raising pattern—blocks apart (left).

Barn Raising pattern—blocks together (right).

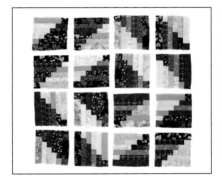
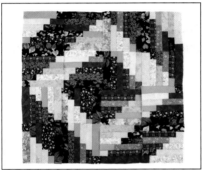

WINDMILL

Windmill pattern—blocks apart (left).

Windmill pattern—blocks together (right).

CONTINUED ON NEXT PAGE

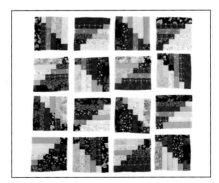
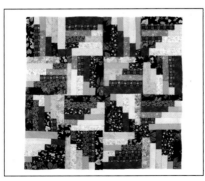

STAR 1

Star 1 pattern—blocks apart (left).

Star 1 pattern—blocks together (right).

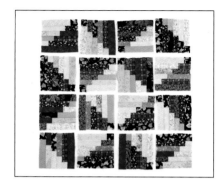
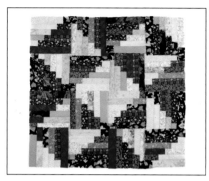

STAR 2

Star 2 pattern—blocks apart (left).

Star 2 pattern—blocks together (right).

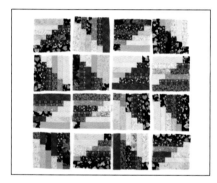
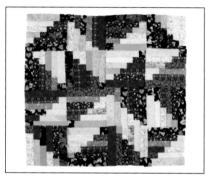

MOUNTAINS

Mountains pattern—blocks apart (left).

Mountains pattern—blocks together (right).

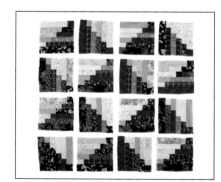
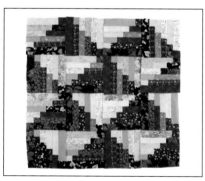

PEAKS AND VALLEYS

Peaks and Valleys pattern—blocks apart (left).

Peaks and Valleys pattern—blocks together (right).

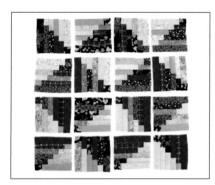 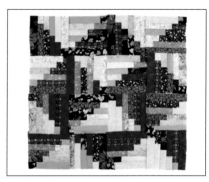

WHIRLIGIG

Whirligig pattern—blocks apart (left).

Whirligig pattern—blocks together (right).

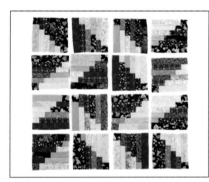 

After you put your Log Cabin blocks together and play with the various layouts, it's time to sew your quilt top together.

Organize Your Work

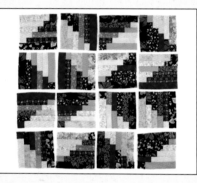

1 As you might guess, sewing your Log Cabin blocks together takes as much care as sewing the individual logs. You could lay your blocks out as you did in the Fence Rail project in Chapter 9 and then pick them up row by row. But if one of them is inadvertently turned as you pin it, your whole quilt-top pattern can be thrown off.

2 I recommend finding a spot where you can lay out all your Log Cabin blocks in your chosen pattern and leave them there while you sew them together. Take the second block from the left in the first row and flip it over onto the first block so that their right sides are together. Pin the blocks together, sew them, press the seam to one side, and return to your layout.

3 Before you pick up the third block in the row, check to be sure you're maintaining the quilt-top pattern by putting your sewed blocks back in place. Then flip the third block on top of the second so it's wrong side up, pin it to its mate, sew them together, press, and return to your layout. Continue in this way across the row. Sew the rows to one another as you complete them, always taking time to make sure they are added in the right order.

As I said before, an iron is one of a quilter's best friends. But this tool requires your attention because the hot, moist heat from a steaming iron can distort fabric. This pressing advice (below) is applicable to the care of any block made of many small pieces.

① While it's tempting to sew all six logs in this Log Cabin block together at once and then press the whole block, the hot steam from an iron accentuates the stretchiness of the fabric, which creates uneven edges.

② For this reason, I recommend pressing each new log as it is added to the block. I know this sounds tedious, but remember that you don't have to make your Log Cabin blocks one at a time. Following the example shown in the photo above, sew several pairs of logs 1 and 2 together, using the technique called chain piecing in Chapter 12.

③ Lay your logs on the ironing board with the log with the greatest proportion of dark fabric facing you. Press the seam while the logs are in this position. This action sets the seam you just made. Now flip the dark fabric up, take a moment to smooth the seam area with your fingers, then press the seam again with the right sides of the fabrics facing you. Remember to move your iron up and down, not side to side.

chapter 11

More Piecing Techniques

In this chapter, we experiment with some small works that integrate the cutting and piecing skills you've learned and expand on them. *Fussy cutting* allows you to extract individual motifs from fabric and use them like photographs in a quilt project. Sashing and posts add drama to a quilt top because they set off individual blocks while lending overall visual support to a quilt-top pattern. Borders call for the same skills as sashing but frame the outside of an entire quilt top. In addition to single fabric borders, this chapter includes instructions for a simple pieced border in a pattern often called Stack of Coins.

Though small, these holiday projects integrate some very important piecing techniques—fussy cutting, sashing and posts, and borders. Before we begin cutting and piecing, let's learn some terminology.

Most of the time, when quilters cut fabric for a project, they slice right through a print. But sometimes you may want to keep a portion of a fabric's print intact. This is especially true with novelty fabrics that feature large motifs that you'd like to use in a quilt top. The poinsettia in the smaller project is a case in point. It was kept intact by a technique called *fussy cutting*. Other important quilting elements such as sashing, posts, and borders are also a part of these projects. We take a closer look at them in the following pages.

The strips of fabric that surround the Pinwheels in this project are called *sashing*. Sashing functions like a picture frame around a individual block or group of blocks in a quilt top. (For information on Pinwheels, see Chapter 13.)

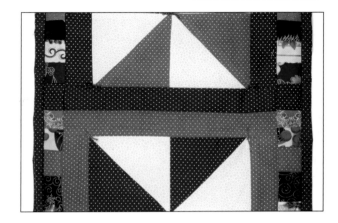

Posts are the small squares situated at the junctions of pieces of sashing or borders. Posts are used in places where vertical strips of sashing or borders meet their horizontal counterparts.

Oftentimes, a quilt top includes a border to complement the blocks in the interior of the quilt. Borders are often long strips of a single fabric. But borders can also be pieced, such as the one around this table runner. This particular *pieced border*, called Stack of Coins, is made from a very simple strip set and gives you a chance to use up some of your accumulating scrap pile.

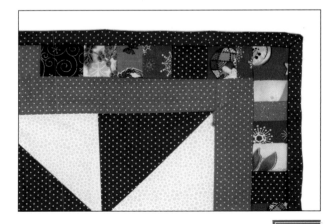

Holiday Projects Overview

The table decorations pictured at the beginning of this chapter originated in my accumulation of Christmas fabrics. To this stash of reds and greens, I added the fabric with the poinsettia motif, and a white-on-white fabric. Approximate fabric requirements for the poinsettia table decoration, featured on this page, are listed below, followed by some general advice for fabric needs if you wish to sew several projects in a similar vein.

WHAT YOU NEED TO KNOW

For these projects, you need to know:

How to true the edge of a piece of fabric and cut strips to a certain size using a rotary cutter, ruler, and mat. (See chapters 5 and 6.)

WHAT YOU WILL LEARN

In these projects, you will learn how to:

Fussy cut fabric in order to use its design elements.
Measure, cut, and fit a border with posts.
Add sashing to a block.

Materials

TOP

¼ yard novelty or large-print fabric for central motif. *Be sure that your yardage includes the entire motif you wish to use.*

BORDER AND BACKING

¼ yard print to complement central motif (green with white dots in example)

POSTS

4 squares, 2 × 2 inches in fabric to complement and contrast with border fabric (red with white dots in example)

BINDING

⅓ yard for straight grain binding (see Chapter 18)

BATTING

Polyester batting measuring 14 × 14 inches (see Chapter 16)

This general fabric advice is useful for when you wish to make several small projects at the same time.

1 If you wish to make more than one project at a time, decide on your theme first. Do you want to celebrate the bright colors of summer? Have you sewn some individual blocks that you want to make into wall hangings? Is there a holiday you wish to celebrate with gifts to friends? Once you make this decision, dive into your stash to see what you have on hand. For these projects, I gathered the scraps of my Christmas fabrics together.

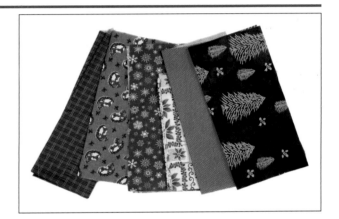

2 Using some large fabric pieces for your backings is helpful. The pieces shown here also appear in the Stack of Coins border.

3 With all this color, you need a neutral fabric to provide a common element in the overall pattern. For sparkling wall hangings, I chose a white-on-white fabric with a print that resembles piles of snowballs. I bought approx. 5 yards—far more than I needed. But it was on sale and you can never have enough fabric in your stash.

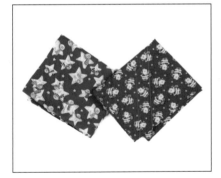

Fussy Cutting

Generally speaking, when you cut strips, you measure them out with your ruler without regard to the print on the fabric. As you roll your rotary cutter along, you slice through flowers or stripes or geometric shapes with abandon. But if you want to focus on a print so that it's preserved whole, you need to *fussy cut* it.

Make a Window

1 Start by taking a general measurement of your selected design element. For example, this poinsettia design is approximately 6 × 6 inches (a).

2 Draw a 6½ × 6½-inch square (the motif size plus seam allowances) on a sheet of plain white paper (b). Cut out the square and keep the frame.

3 Lay the frame over your chosen design element. Move it gently from side to side and top to bottom in order to decide exactly how you wish the design element to appear once it's sewn in place. Keep the sides of your frame parallel to the outside edges of your fabric so that your fussy cutting will be in line with the grain of your fabric. Once that decision is made, use a nonpermanent fabric marker such as chalk to mark the corners of your window on the fabric.

Cut Out Your Print

1 Generally, fabric is printed in a regular rhythm so that its print appears over and over again in the same intervals. This means that you can often cut multiple design elements at the same time using the fussy cutting method. Notice, in the fabric on the right, that the poinsettias alternate with smaller red flowers. Since you want to keep the poinsettia, you will cut the fabric in a way that preserves this design.

2 Lay your ruler on the fabric, lining it up with two of the corner marks that you just made, and in the direction of the poinsettia print. Notice that the print motif is all on one side of the ruler.

3 Make your first cut. Move your ruler to the other corner marks you made. Pause to be absolutely sure your ruler is in the proper location. Make your second cut. Turn the fabric strip 90 degrees and carefully separate the design elements from one another. When you are done, measure the motifs to be certain they are the right size.

Sashing with Posts

Sashing, posts, and borders call on the skills you learned in chapters 6 and 9, cutting squares and strips. *Sashing* is used to frame individual blocks in the interior of a quilt. *Posts* are squares of fabric that sit at the junction of the vertical and horizontal parts of sashing or borders. You don't *have* to include posts in either sashing or a border.

Add Sashing with Posts

① Add sashing pieces to the outside of a block or square two at a time. Start with the sides of this poinsettia square. Before you cut your sashing pieces, measure your square or block across its center (not on the edge where the fabric could be stretched). You will use this measurement to cut your sashing.

② Cut a strip of your sashing fabric 2 inches wide. Unfold the strip and turn it 90 degrees. Cut two pieces to the same length as the sides of your square, and two the same length as the top and bottom of the square.

③ Attach a piece of sashing to the top and bottom of your square. Use the pressing technique described in Chapter 10 to press the seams of your sashing pieces to one side.

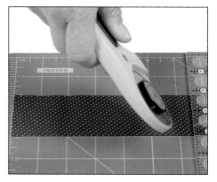

Add Posts

1 Generally, sashing and border pieces are added to a quilt two at a time: the top and bottom then the two remaining sides. If you are going to add posts, they are attached to the second set of sashing or border pieces. Posts are squares cut to the same width as the sashing or border. In this example, our border is 2 inches wide so you need to cut four posts 2 x 2 inches.

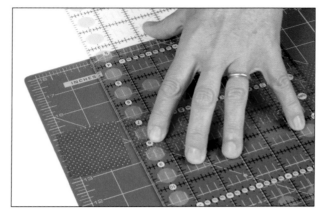

2 Attach a post to both ends of one piece of sashing or border.

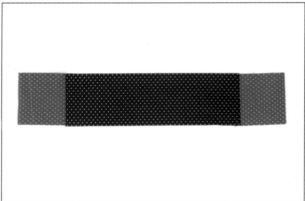

3 Attach your sashing and post unit to the top of your square. Be very sure to align the seams. Attach the second piece of sashing and posts to the bottom. Press the seams to one side.

Sashing without Posts

Sometimes you want to frame a block without using posts. This dramatic framing effect allows a block to visually float in a pool of color.

Plain Sashing

1 Measure the length of your square or block, as you did in Step 1 in the previous section. Cut two pieces of sashing or border to this measurement and sew them to the top and bottom of your block or square, as you did in Step 3 in the previous section.

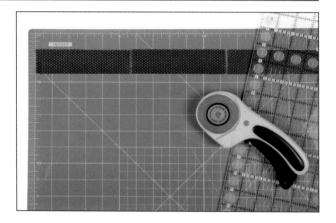

2 When the first two pieces of sashing are added to your square or block (a), measure across the whole unit—the block or square plus the sashing. Cut two strips of fabric to the same size as this measurement. (All the sashing strips in this project are cut 2 inches wide.)

3 Attach these two pieces of sashing to the top and bottom of your block or square (b). Press the seams to one side.

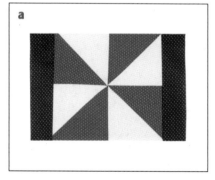

a

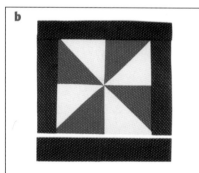

b

Borders serve many purposes in a quilt. Their main task is to frame a quilt top that needs a frame. They also can add more color to a quilt top, such as the border in the following section called Stack of Coins, or extend a quilt's length or width to cover a bed. They even can repeat a color or design in a quilt top as a way of unifying a quilt, such as the project in Chapter 14, setting on point. Then again, some quilts, such as the Log Cabin in Chapter 10, look just fine without a border at all.

Choosing Border Fabrics

If you have some potential border fabrics in your stash, lay your quilt top on them one at a time then step back to study the effect. Borders can be more than one fabric so try two. If you don't have any candidates for a border or want to try something new, take your completed quilt top to your local shop to test fabrics for the border or your work.

Squares quilt on orange fabric.

Squares quilt on green fabric.

Squares quilt on both green and orange.

Add a Border

Borders are added to the outside of a quilt in essentially the same way that sashing is added to the outside of a block or square—with two essential differences in measuring and attaching.

1 As you piece your blocks and rows together to form a quilt top, the outside edges of your work get stretched with handling. For this reason, you should measure for a border across the middle of the quilt top. To begin, lay your tape measure down the middle of the quilt from top to bottom. Cut two pieces of your border fabric to this measurement. There are two borders on this quilt. The inner, green border is cut 1½ inches wide. The outer, orange border is 3½ inches wide. Double borders are added to a quilt one at a time and the procedures are the same for both.

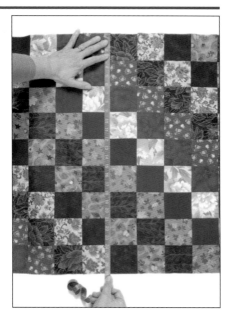

2 Remember that you sew a quilt top to its border, not the other way around. Starting in the middle of each piece, which you can mark with pins, attach your top and border together with the border fabric on top. Pin the middle, then the two ends, then back to the middle until the whole border is pinned.

3 Once your side border pieces are attached, measure your quilt from side to side across the middle—including the borders. Cut two pieces of your border fabric to this length and attach them to the sides, pinning the border pieces on top of the quilt top. If you wish to include posts, follow the instructions given in "Sashing with Posts," discussed earlier in this chapter. If you wish to attach a second border fabric, as in this example, follow the same steps as above.

Borders do not have to be single pieces of fabric. Many quilts include elaborately pieced borders. Here's a fun one to try. Remember the strip set lessons you learned in chapters 9 and 10? Stack of Coins is an extension of these same strip set skills.

① Stack of Coins takes advantage of scrap fabric but can also be made from yardage. Strips may be the same width, but it's more exciting if the widths vary. For this project, cut at least 16 strips of various fabrics into various widths between ¾ and 1½ inches.

② If they are not approximately the same length, cut your strips to match the length of your shortest piece. Organize them on your sewing table according to color.

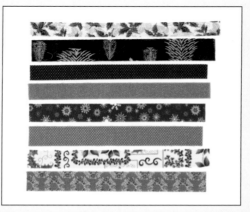

③ Attach strips to one another either randomly or in a set order. Press seams toward the darker fabrics one or two at a time with the technique you used in Chapter 10 with the Log Cabin blocks. Do not make a strip set longer than you can easily fit on your cutting mat.

④ True one edge of your strip set, then cut a 2-inch strip from it. Measure your border pieces according to the instructions earlier in this chapter. If you need a longer Stack of Coins, join one strip to another to achieve length. Cut to size as you would a single piece of fabric.

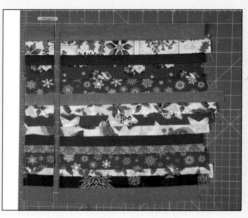

chapter 12

Four Patch and Nine Patch

So far, you've learned how to cut squares, determine the size of various pieces in a quilt, make strip sets, and add sashing, posts, and borders to a quilt project. Before you move on to triangles and crazy quilting, there are a few more tricks to learn about piecing.

Create Four-Patch Blocks with Strip Sets

Four-Patch blocks appear in more quilt tops than probably any other block. Generally speaking, Four-Patch blocks contain both repetition and contrast because two of the four squares are of the same fabric or color family while the other two squares are cut from contrasting colors. The blocks at right and center are examples. At other times, Four-Patch blocks are made of two matching pairs of squares, such as the block on the left.

Four-Patch Block Composition

Any time you see repetition in a quilt, the quilter probably used a strip set to create it. The repetition in this Four Patch is a clue that it is made from one strip set.

When you take the two matching pairs of this Four Patch apart, you can see how they were formed from the same strip set of two fabrics. The finished size of this Four Patch is 4 × 4 inches which means that the finished size of each square in it is 2 × 2 inches. Using the same quilting math featured in Chapter 6, you can calculate that the unfinished size of each square is 2½ × 2½ inches.

Make Four-Patch Blocks

1 To make these Four-Patch blocks, cut strips from different fabrics to your desired finished width plus ½ inch for the seam allowances. In this case, these strips are 2½ inches wide.

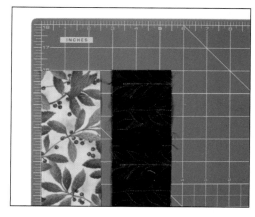

2 Once the two strips are cut, sew them together in pairs then cut your individual pieces to the correct unfinished size of your Four-Patch block. In this case, the blocks are cut 2½ inches wide.

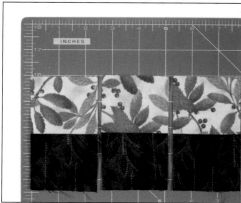

3 To finish the Four-Patch block, take two pieces from your strip set, rotate one of them 180 degrees (see photo). Lay one strip set piece on top of the other, right sides facing, and sew them together matching the seams. If you sew several Four-Patch blocks at the same time, turn to the next page to learn how to chain piece them together.

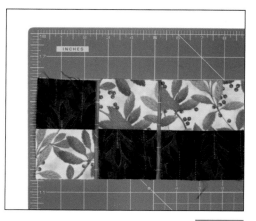

As you may have gathered by this time, if you plan to make a number of the same piece at the same time, you will probably look for a way to streamline that process. Chain piecing works splendidly when you put a lot of Four-Patch blocks together at the same time. This same sewing-machine technique can be used in several different areas of quilting. Chain piecing saves time and thread.

1 Once your individual Four-Patch pieces are cut from a strip set, pin them all together in pairs ready for sewing as shown in (a).

2 When you chain piece, you do it just as you would sew any seam. But when you reach the end of the first pair of pieces, do not raise the presser foot of your machine (b).

3 Feed your next pinned pair of pieces under your presser foot. They should rest close to the pair you just sewed. Continue sewing. Your needle should make one to three stitches between your pinned pieces. After you seam the second pair, don't raise the presser foot but feed your next set under the needle. Continue in this way until all of your paired sets are sewed.

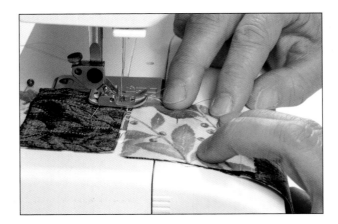

TIP

While there is no limit to the number of pieces you can chain stitch in a row, keep in mind that the weight of your completed pieces will pull on your sewing after a while. When this happens, start a new chain.

④ When you are done, your chained Four-Patch blocks will be attached in the fashion pictured at right. Take them to your ironing board, lay them down with the darkest fabric on top, and press them following the instructions for pressing in Chapter 10.

⑤ Once the blocks are pressed, use scissors to clip the sewing threads that connect the blocks together.

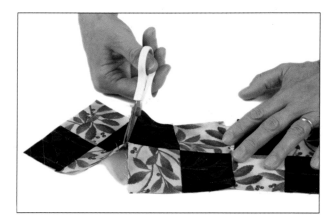

TIP

If you want to make Four-Patch blocks from more than two colors, decide what pairs of colors you want in your blocks then create strip sets from each pair of colors, cut your pieces, and then join them to one another as described above.

Create Nine-Patch Blocks with Strip Sets

Remember the game of Tic Tac Toe from your childhood? Nine-Patch blocks are Tic Tac Toe in fabric, three rows of three squares. You create Nine-Patch blocks by combining two different strip sets.

Nine-Patch Block Composition

Traditionally, Nine-Patch blocks include two different repeating patterns. The most common pattern is the block featured on the left with all four corner squares and the center square of the same fabric. The second most common repetition is a block with the four corner squares of the same fabric, the fabric between the corner squares is the same, and the center square of a third fabric, like the Nine-Patch block on the right.

Note: *Some quilt patterns call for Nine-Patch or Four-Patch blocks constructed with patterns that don't repeat fabrics in the way described here in order to achieve a specific visual effect. These specialty patterns often contain instructions for strip sets so the techniques described here still apply.*

If you divide a Nine-Patch block into its three basic parts (a)—top squares, middle squares, bottom squares— you see that the block is made of two strip sets, one for the top and bottom set of squares, another for the middle set of squares.

Using this block (b) as an example, the finished size of the block is 6 × 6 inches. The finished size of each square in the block is 2 × 2 inches. With seam allowances, you get squares in the unfinished size of 2½ × 2½ inches.

Make Nine-Patch Blocks

1 The top- and bottom-row sequence of this block is green/yellow/green. For this strip set, cut three strips of fabric 2½ inches wide, and sew them to one another in the same sequence—green/yellow/green. Press the seams toward the darker fabric then cut sets of strips measuring 2½ inches wide. For every Nine-Patch block, you need two sets of squares from this strip set. These blocks are used in the tablecloth project later in this chapter.

2 The middle-row sequence for this block is the opposite of the other two: yellow/green/yellow. This strip set requires two strips of yellow fabric 2½ inches wide and one strip of green the same width. Sew them to one another in this sequence— yellow/green/yellow. Press the seams toward the darker fabric, then cut sets of squares from the strip set measuring 2½ inches wide. For every Nine-Patch block, you need one set of squares from this strip set.

3 Sew a green/yellow/green strip set to both sides of the yellow/green/yellow. Make sure you align the seams that join the squares to one another. Press the seams that join the rows in opposite directions from one another.

Combine Blocks in a Tablecloth Project

Now that you've learned many of the basic skills of cutting and piecing, try your hand at combining different small blocks into one larger block. This project is a tablecloth created to fit a square table measuring 50 × 50 inches with a 5-inch overhang on all four sides. The fabric requirements and measurements given are specific for this size table.

WHAT YOU NEED TO KNOW

For this project you need to know:

How to true the edge of a piece of fabric and cut strips to a certain size using a rotary cutter, ruler, and mat. (See chapters 5 and 6.)

How to cut squares from a strip of fabric. (See Chapter 6.)

How to create a strip set. (See Chapter 9.)

Organize blocks into a quilt top before sewing. (See Chapter 7.)

Create Four-Patch and Nine-Patch blocks with strip sets. Chain piece.

WHAT YOU WILL LEARN

In this project, you will learn how to:

Surround blocks with sashing.

Make pieced sashing with strip sets.

TOP

1 yard of yellow leaf fabric for small Nine Patch blocks and pieced border

1 yard green leaf fabric for small Nine Patch blocks and pieced border

½ yard of leaf print for center square in large Nine Patch blocks and pieced border

1 yard of brick red fabric for alternate squares in large Nine Patch blocks

SASHING

½ yard dark green solid for sashing

BORDER

In addition to the fabric used in the pieced border: 2 yards unbleached muslin

Note: There are no posts, backing, batting, or binding in this project.

The large blocks in the center of this tablecloth are in a pattern often referred to as Nine in Nine. Look closely. Notice that the squares in the corners of each of these large blocks are the smaller Nine-Patch blocks created in the previous pages. The center square of the larger block is of a different fabric than any of the other squares. The squares in the middle of each side are a single piece of fabric. When single fabric squares are inserted between blocks made of smaller pieces of fabric, the single piece fabric squares are called *alternate squares*.

Notice the two different levels of sashing in the tablecloth. The first is the dark green surrounding each of the four large blocks. The second is the neutral muslin framing the green. Likewise, there are two borders: a pieced one made of fabrics found in the Nine-in-Nine blocks and an outside border of unbleached muslin. It is not quilted or bound. The outer edge of the tablecloth is hemmed by hand.

So this tablecloth combines squares from Chapter 6, Nine-Patch blocks created from strip sets (Chapter 9 and this chapter), sashing (Chapter 11), and pieced sashing (later in this chapter). I encourage you, as you gain confidence in your quilting skills, to try your hand at combining various elements in a project of your own design.

A "Nine-in-Nine" tablecloth. Finished size: 60 × 60 inches.

Select Your Colors for the Tablecloth

Sometimes quilt projects begin with a pattern. Sometimes they begin with fabric. For example, this tablecloth begins with the two leaf-print fabrics featured in the small Nine-Patch blocks. They are of the same print pattern but their color schemes are different. Because I routinely buy more of a fabric that I really like so I'll have extra, I purchased a yard of each.

The large size of this third leaf-print fabric calls for using it as an alternate block so that more of its lovely design can be appreciated. Following the same idea as above, I purchased a yard of this fabric. The half-yard of brick colored tone-on-tone fabric is from my stash. The color blends well with the three leaf prints.

Since the colors of the fabrics in the large blocks are vibrant, I think they call for an equally saturated color for sashing that can frame and hold the large blocks together visually. The deep green is chosen for that purpose. And muslin is always a good choice in a quilt when you want to separate design elements. Muslin neutrals in a quilt act much like rests do in music.

① Following the instructions given in the previous Nine-Patch section, make sixteen Nine-Patch blocks. When they are complete, measure them to be certain they are the same size, 6½ inches × 6½ inches. If necessary, true their edges but be very careful to take only slivers of fabric from the edges.

② Cut sixteen squares from the fabric you chose for the alternate blocks that appear between the corner Nine-Patch blocks. These alternate blocks should be exactly the same size as the Nine-Patch blocks. Cut four squares from the fabric you chose for the centers of the large blocks. These should also be the same size as the Nine-Patch blocks.

③ Attach Nine-Patch blocks to the right and left sides of two alternate blocks. Sew an alternate block to the right and left sides of the center block. Sew a Nine-Patch unit to the top and bottom of the unit containing the center block, taking care to match the seams between the blocks.

Note: To minimize the bulk of the seams in the finished tablecloth, press all your seams open instead of to one side or the other. Bulky seams make the surface of the finished project uneven and liable to tip over small glasses or other lightweight objects set on a table.

Sashing between Blocks

When you add sashing between blocks, it dramatizes the color and pattern of the block. Matching seams is very important during this step, and there are some ways to help this happen smoothly.

1 Once your large blocks are complete, measure them on all four sides to be certain they are square and the same size as one another. As you put pieces together in a quilt, this accuracy becomes more and more important. The sashing is cut 2½ inches wide, the same width as the individual squares in the small patch. (a)

2 Cut two strips of fabric to the same size as one side of your large blocks (b). In this example, these strips of sashing measure 2½ × 18½ inches.

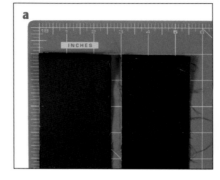

3 Sew a large block to both sides of each piece of sashing. Be sure the seams you make are of the same size. Press the seams open, and continue with instructions on the next page.

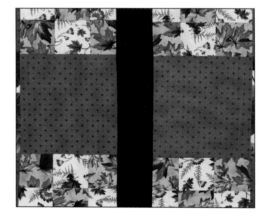

TIP

When you design your own quilt tops, cut your design elements to the same size or multiples of the same size. For example, the strips of sashing in this tablecloth are the same width (2½ inches) as the individual blocks of the small Nine Patch. Visually, this gives your quilt consistency and it is easier to fit pieces together.

④ Measure these new units to be certain they are the same size. Cut one piece of 2½-inch sashing to this size. Attach only one of your large block units to the sashing. Press the seam open.

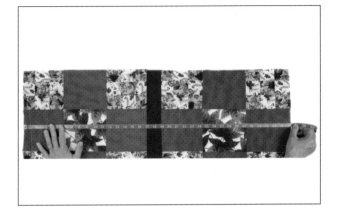

⑤ I stress careful measurement and sewing throughout this project. This constant check for accuracy ensures that your completed project satisfies you visually and lays flat on the table. When this seam is complete, the edges of the large blocks must be right across from one another. This is how you do that:

Turn your large block and sashing unit right side down on a firm surface. Take your ruler and align its edge with the seam between a large block and the first piece of sashing that you attached. Your ruler should extend over the second piece of sashing.

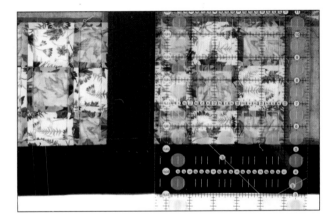

⑥ Select a marking tool with a fine point and mark the line of the seam across the second piece of sashing. Align the ruler with the seam that attaches your second large block to your first piece of sashing and mark the line of this seam as well. These lines provide an alignment guide for your next seam.

CONTINUED ON NEXT PAGE

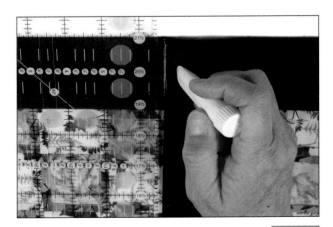

7 When you pin the second large block unit to this piece of sashing, start by aligning its seams with the marks you made on the sashing. Before you sew, take a moment to flip your project right side up to make sure the seams of the first large block unit align with the seam lines of the second large block unit. Sew the seam. Press the seam open.

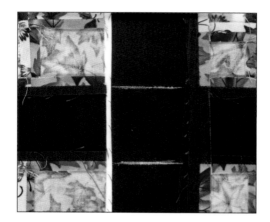

8 Measure the top and bottom edges of your four-block unit. Cut two 2½ inch wide strips of sashing to this measurement. Attach these sashing pieces to the top and bottom of your large block. Once these are attached and the seams pressed open, measure the left and right sides, cut strips of sashing to fit, and attach them. Press the seams open.

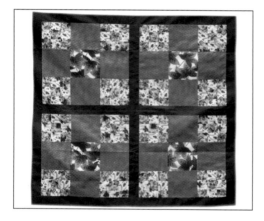

9 There are different shades of muslin to choose from in quilting. Of the three pictured here, the darkest complements the other colors best. Use the same method as above to add a second layer of sashing in muslin. The second layer of sashing in this project is cut 6½ inches wide, the same width as the alternate squares in the large block units.

Note: *For more instructions on sashing, please see Chapter 11.*

Like the Stack of Coins border in Chapter 11, this tablecloth border is pieced. But the size and shape of the pieces does not vary and replicates the size and shape of the same fabrics in the tablecloth's top.

❶ Cut 2½-inch strips from the leaf fabrics in the tablecloth top. Here, I did not include the brick-colored fabric because its color would overwhelm the muted values of the leaf print fabrics. Sew the strips together in any order, just don't put two of the same fabric together (a).

❷ I cut this strip unit into 2½-inch pieces (b) in order to repeat the size of the squares in the small Nine-Patch blocks in the center of the quilt.

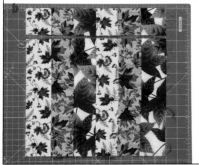

❸ Once the 2½-inch pieces are cut in the step above, sew them to one another to form a long ribbon of squares. Measure the top and bottom of your project, make two ribbons of pieced border to this size, and attach them to the muslin sashing. Measure the left and right sides of your project. Make two ribbons of pieced border to this size, and attach them to your project. Attach an outside border of muslin to your tablecloth if desired. The finished width of the outside border on this project is 2 inches.

 TIP

Pieced borders can be a great place to experiment with color. Instead of repeating fabrics in a quilt top, try using fabrics that complement your color scheme.

All beginning quilters experience some frustrating moments as they learn this craft. You may be in a hurry and miscut a strip by a quarter inch. Your attention may drift as you sew a seam. Sometimes you don't know exactly what happened but the pieces of a project just don't come out the right size. My goal throughout this book is to give you the tools to learn this wonderful craft and the encouragement to learn it. That's why it's important to talk about mistakes so you know that every quilter learns this way.

This tablecloth project was originally planned with six large blocks (such as the one pictured below) so that it would fit my dining-room table with its leaf. It was just before Thanksgiving and I had the bright idea of adorning my table with a cloth of my own design and creation. Of course, with just a few days to go before the holiday, I was in a hurry.

Since I'd made many a Nine-Patch block before, I didn't feel the necessity to measure the completed blocks before I combined them with the alternate squares. In fact, it wasn't until I attached the large blocks to the dark green sashing that I realized something was very wrong. I detached the large blocks from the sashing, certain that I could right the wrong with a little trimming.

But the square would not become square no matter how hard I tried. I'm still not sure what I did wrong except that I was in a hurry. So the tablecloth shrank to four large blocks, just the right size to cover my table without its leaf. And what about the unsquare Nine Patch? Well, it made a dandy potholder. The center of this potholder is a half-square Triangle (Chapter 13) with a border on only two sides (Chapter 11 and this chapter). Before you make your own potholders, please turn to Chapter 16 for important information about batting.

chapter 13

Triangles

While a number of quilt patterns consist of only squares and rectangles, the third shape—the triangle—gives a quilter a wider range of patterns to choose from. Triangles are a bit of a challenge to get just right but with a little practice, you'll do just fine. Before you know it, you'll be sewing stars—literally.

Half-Square Triangle Challenges

Of all the angled pieces in quilting, the half-square triangle is the most common and arguably the most versatile. It appears in numerous quilt-block patterns such as Pinwheel, Bear's Paw, Tree of Life, and any number of stars. This triangle can be used all on its own to great effect or combined with quilting standards such as Nine Patch or Fence Rail. Depending on your fabric choice it can add surprise and interest to any quilt top.

As you learned in the previous chapters, one of the most important considerations in quilting is seam allowance. If you want to end up with a 4-inch square, you need to begin with a 4½-inch square in order to account for the ¼-inch seam allowance on all four sides. In triangles, this seam allowance figuring gets a different twist because you have three sides, not four, and one of them is not the same length as the other two.

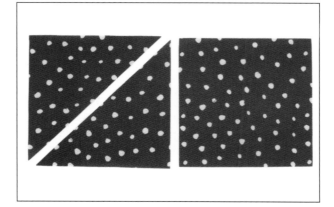

Another challenge with triangles is making sure their points are all sharp and visible when they are combined with other pieces of fabric. The triangle point on the top right is lost in a seam. The triangle point in the bottom left appears to be floating because there is a space between it and the seam. The triangle point on the top left sits right where it should. These challenges will be met as you sew Pinwheels in the following pages.

1 Half-square triangles begin as squares of fabric. But instead of a ¼-inch seam allowance, these squares are cut with a ⅞-inch seam allowance. In this example, you want to end up with a half-square triangle block that measures 3 × 3 inches. So the square's unfinished size is 3⅞ × 3⅞ inches.

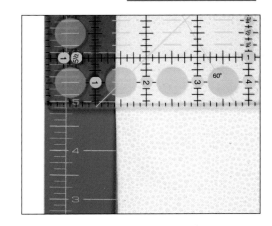

2 Half-square triangles are most often sewn together in pairs of two fabrics with high contrast. In this example, you make four pinwheel blocks and put them together in a small wall hanging. Sixteen half-square triangles are in this piece, each with a 3 × 3-inch finished size. To begin, choose two fabrics with high contrast. Cut eight squares from each fabric measuring 3⅞ × 3⅞ inches.

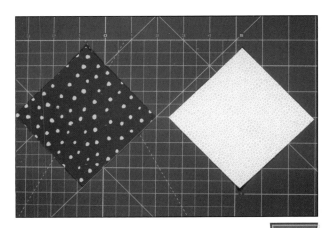

3 Half-square triangles can be made in a few different ways, but I find this method to be the easiest and most accurate. Once you cut your squares, lay them on your cutting mat, aligning two opposite corners of each square with a measuring line.

CONTINUED ON NEXT PAGE

④ Lay your ruler on the measuring line of your mat and cut your fabric pairs in half diagonally. Make sure you cut through the points of the squares. *Accurate cutting is one of the keys to making triangles.*

Before you sew, pair your triangles so that you have one from each fabric. In this example, the two triangles on the bottom are swapped with one another so that you end up with two polka dot and white fabric pairs.

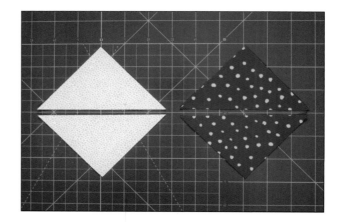

⑤ Pin your pairs of cut triangles together and then sew them together along the diagonal cut you just made. If I make a number of half-square triangles at the same time, I chain piece them (see Chapter 12). Press the seams toward the darker fabric.

⑥ When you're done sewing, all of your triangle units will have small tabs showing beyond the edge of the fabric. Use your scissors to cut these tabs flush with the fabric edge. When you pin pieces of fabric to one another, you have a tendency to start at one end and pin/sew to the other. If you do this with triangles that have not been evened in this way, the triangles will not line up with one another.

Note: *Stitching your seams slowly is always a good idea in quilting, especially with triangles. This one practice will probably do more to increase your accuracy than anything else you can do.*

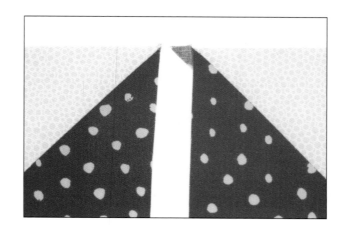

7 Take four of your half-square triangles and lay them out in the pinwheel formation pictured here. As you sew them together, you're going to make ¼-inch seams. Starting at the top, sew the left half-square triangle unit to its partner on the right. Do the same for the pair on the bottom. Press the seams to one side.

8 Before you join the two pairs to one another, take a moment to turn one of the pairs over and examine the back. Do you see the place where the vertical seam that joined the two units crosses the diagonal seam? When you join these units in a row, your joining seam must cross this junction in order for all of your triangle points to be displayed properly.

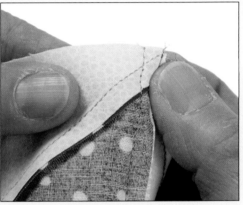

9 Pin your two pairs together, making sure you have them aligned correctly. It's very easy to get triangles turned in the wrong direction so double check them before you sew. Be sure your center seams line up with one another. Sew your two pairs together. Press this final seam *open* to reduce bulk.

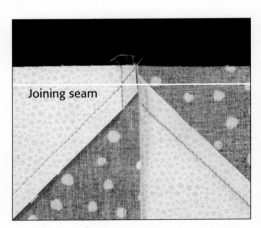

Joining seam

10 Make three more pinwheels and join them to one another as pictured. I finished this wall hanging with a 2-inch border of the white fabric (see Chapter 12), hand tied it (see Chapter 17) and then bound it with the blue fabric (see Chapter 18).

North Star Wall Hanging

In Chapter 10, you learned how to use the same Log Cabin blocks to make several different quilt-top patterns, just by playing with the contrast between dark and light fabrics. Half-square triangles lend themselves to this same sort of play. This North Star wall hanging uses the same number of half-square triangle units as the pinwheels in the previous section. Historically, the North Star pattern was used as a code in quilts used to guide runaway slaves on the Underground Railroad.

1. Choose two fabrics with high contrast. Cut eight 3⅞ × 3⅞-inch squares from each fabric. Cut and sew sixteen half-triangle square units according to steps 3, 4, and 5 in the previous section. Press the seams to one side; cut off the tabs. Lay the completed units out in star formation (a).

2. Starting with the top row, sew the half-triangle units to one another (b). Make sure you turn them the right way before you sew. You might press all of the row seams open to minimize bulk.

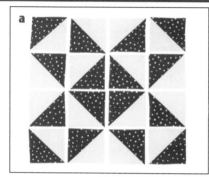
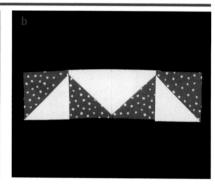

3. Join the four rows to one another, working from top to bottom, to complete the star. I added 2-inch strips of white fabric as borders to this piece, following the instructions for borders in Chapter 11. Tie at every point where four triangle points meet, following instructions in Chapter 17, and add backing, batting, and binding according to chapters 16 and 18.

When you add other fabric shapes to a block with half-square triangles, the possibilities for new and exciting patterns are almost endless. You can begin that experimentation here with a Pinwheel Star and then continue with a second project in the next section.

1 This star pattern features twelve half-square triangle units and four full squares in the corners. Choose two fabrics with high contrast. Cut six squares of each fabric measuring $3\frac{7}{8} \times 3\frac{7}{8}$ inches. Following the instructions for sewing half-square triangles earlier in this chapter, cut and sew twelve half-square triangle units. Press the seams to one side. Cut four squares of your light fabric for the corners, $3\frac{1}{2} \times 3\frac{1}{2}$ inches. Lay the pieces out in the formation pictured.

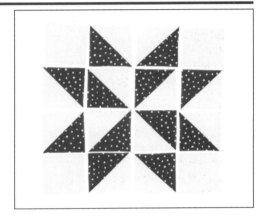

2 Starting with the top row, join the pieces to one another, making sure the triangle units are going in the right direction. Join the rows to one another, working from top to bottom. Make sure seams line up and that your joining seams are accurately sewn so that your points are all visible. Press the joining seams open to reduce bulk.

TIP

Try your hand at star creation. Sew a number of half-square triangle units, eight to sixteen, and experiment with them by combining them in different patterns. Add some alternate squares or a Fence Rail block or a Nine Patch to see what combinations you like.

Pinwheel Star Quilt Project

This quilt features pinwheel blocks cozied right up to one another and highlighted with alternate squares in a soft salmon color. Notice that each pinwheel is actually made in a Nine-Patch formation (see Chapter 12) consisting of four half-triangle units and five squares, one in the center and one in each corner.

WHAT YOU NEED TO KNOW

For this project, you need to know:

> How to cut fabric to size with a rotary cutter, ruler, and mat. (See chapters 5 and 6.)
> How to organize pattern pieces in rows for sewing. (See chapters 6, 7, and 8.)
> How to select fabrics with contrast for a quilt top. (See Chapter 4.)

WHAT YOU WILL EXPERIENCE

In this project, you will experience how to:

> Cut and sew triangles to the correct size.
> Preserve a triangle's points.
> Combine squares and triangles in the same block for dramatic effect.

Materials

TOP

¾ yard dark fabric

¾ yard light fabric

½ yard midtone fabric

BACKING

1½ yards of one of the fabrics used in the quilt top, muslin or a cotton of your choice

BINDING

¼ yard

BATTING

Crib-sized, 45 × 60, low loft in cotton, polyester, or blend

This project was quilted using the Quilt-as-You-Go method described in Chapter 17.

Pinwheel Star quilt. Finished size: 34 × 40 inches.

CONTINUED ON NEXT PAGE

1 From your midtone fabric, cut forty-two squares measuring 3½ × 3½ inches. From the dark fabric, cut fifteen squares measuring 3½ × 3½ inches. From the light fabric, cut fifteen squares measuring 3½ × 3½ inches. Separate the squares in piles according to fabric.

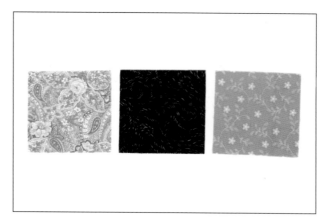

2 Cut thirty-six squares measuring 3⅞ × 3⅞ inches from the light and the dark fabrics. Following the instructions for making half-square triangle units, cut and sew seventy-two units from the light and dark fabrics. Press the seams toward the dark fabric. Cut off the tabs.

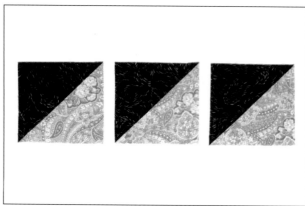

3 This quilt is 11 squares across in 13 rows. In order to make sure the half-square triangle units are slanted in the right direction, lay all of the pieces out at the same time. The easiest way to do this is to use the photographs at right and on the previous page as a diagram and lay your pieces out accordingly. Starting in the top-left corner, join the first two pieces then add each new square one at a time. Press these seams open. Join the rows to one another as you complete them. Press these seams to one side.

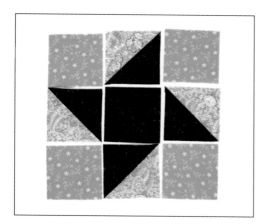

While not as common as half-square triangles, quarter-square triangles add another design dimension to quilting. They give you the flexibility to combine triangles from three different fabrics in the same block. Quarter-square triangles are also used in a technique called *setting on point*, covered in Chapter 14. Like half-square triangles, quarter-square triangles can be used by themselves in a pattern called Hourglass or they can be combined with squares to make Ohio Star, both of which are featured in the table runner project following this section.

As you might suspect, quarter-square triangles begin with one square cut in four pieces. As with half-square triangles, this extra cutting and piecing requires more fabric for seam allowances. With quarter-square triangles, you need to add 1¼ inches to your finished size in order for your units to come out right. For example, if you want a quarter-square unit in a 4-inch finished size, you need to start with squares cut to 5¼ inches.

Quarter-square triangles in Ohio Star pattern.

Quarter-square triangles in Hourglass pattern.

CONTINUED ON NEXT PAGE

Hourglass Pattern

1 You're going to make two quarter-square triangle units, one with two fabrics and one with three. Let's begin with a two-fabric unit. Cut two squares 5¼ × 5¼ inches. Lay them on your cutting mat, just as you would for a half-square triangle, and cut them in half diagonally. Sew the light and dark halves together, press the seams toward the dark fabric and cut off the tabs.

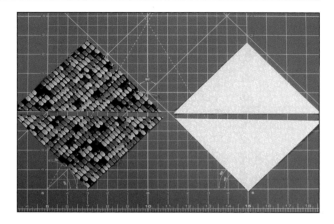

2 Lay these two units on your mat and cut them across the second diagonal, as shown.

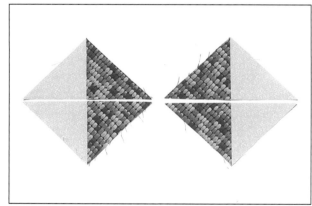

> ### TIP
>
> When you cut your quarter-square units in Step 2 above, you will cut across the seams you made in step one. Take some extra time to be sure you are cutting from point to point and that your ruler does not move as your rotary cutter crosses the seam.

3 Take one half of each unit and swap them with one another so that you end up with pairs that are mirror images of one another, as shown.

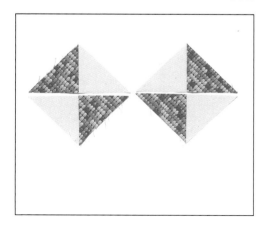

④ Carefully align the seams and sew these pairs together. Press this seam open to reduce bulk. In quilting, quarter-square triangles of two fabrics in this configuration are called the *Hourglass pattern.*

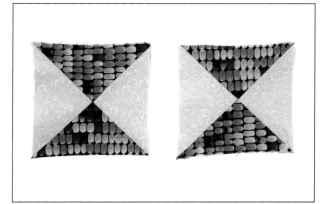

⑤ Hourglass blocks show up in quilts all by themselves but they are most often found in combination with other quilting elements. They often appear in pieced borders or pieced sashings. They can be configured so that fabrics of the same tone are aligned, as in the illustration on the top or they may be juxtaposed so that the colors alternate between dark and light, as in the illustration on the bottom.

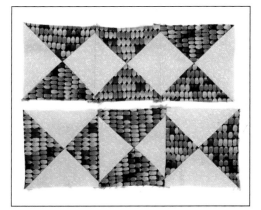

TIP

As with so many quilting patterns, the Hourglass block needs fabrics with a lot of contrast. Before you plunge into a quilt project that uses this pattern, make a test block to be sure your fabrics have the contrast you need.

Quarter-Square Triangle Block with Three Fabrics

If you want to make a quarter-square triangle unit with three fabrics, then choose fabrics with good contrast. In this unit, one of the fabrics appears twice, the other two appear once.

1 For this example, the light fabric appears twice. To make a block with a 4-inch finished size, cut two squares of your repeating fabric 5¼ × 5¼ inches. Cut one square of the same size from each of the other two fabrics (a).

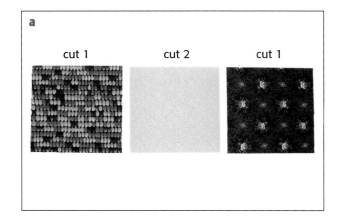

a

cut 1   cut 2   cut 1

2 Following instructions in the previous section, cut your squares in half diagonally (b). Pair up the cut triangles so that one piece of your repeating fabric is in each pair. Sew these pairs together and press the seams to one side.

You will have four units of half-square triangles when you complete this step.

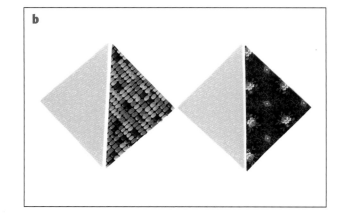

b

3 Lay your sewn pairs back on the cutting mat and cut in half diagonally. Now swap one half of each unit with another so that you end up with blocks that each include three fabrics. The repeating fabrics should be opposite one another. Sew these pairs together and press the seams open.

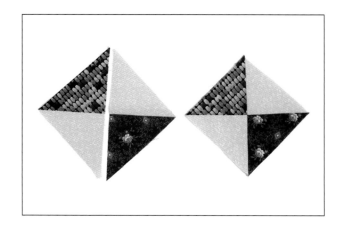

Ohio Star Table Runner with Hourglass Border

The pattern called Ohio Star that's featured in this table runner combines squares with two types of quarter-square triangles: one with three fabrics and a two-fabric hourglass block that's part of the border at the top and bottom. To add interest, the predominant color in the three Ohio Star blocks changes from dark to light and back again.

MAKE THE TABLE RUNNER

1 For this project, you need ½ yard each of a light fabric, a dark fabric, and 1 yard of a decorative or midtone fabric that is used for the binding and backing in addition to its portion of the top of the table runner. Cut five squares of light fabric, three squares of the decorative or midtone fabric, and four squares of the dark fabric 5¼ × 5¼ inches. Do not cut strips for the hourglass border until you complete the Ohio Star blocks.

2 Following the previous section's instructions, cut and sew eight quarter-triangle units with four squares of dark fabric, two squares of light fabric, and two squares of the midtone fabric cut in Step 1 (a). Press all seams toward the darker fabric.

3 Following the previous section's instructions, cut and sew four quarter-triangle units with two squares of the light fabric, one square of the dark, and one square of the midtone fabric. Press all seams toward the darker fabric (b).

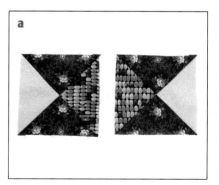

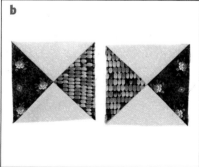

a

b

CONTINUED ON NEXT PAGE

④ Cut nine squares of light fabric 4½ × 4½ inches. Cut six squares of dark fabric to the same measurement. Lay one of the light squares on your worktable. This is the center square for the middle star in the table runner. Arrange the four predominantly light quarter-square triangles on the four sides of the square with the midtone fabric abutting the square. Take four squares of the dark fabric and lay them in the empty corners made by the star, as shown in the photograph. Join these pieces together in rows, working from left to right and top to bottom. Press the seams open to reduce bulk.

⑤ Lay two squares of the dark fabric on your worktable. These are the center squares for the other two stars in this project. Arrange the predominantly dark quarter-square triangle units around the outsides of these two squares with the midtone fabric abutting the center square. Place a square of light fabric cut in Step 4 in the empty corners made by the stars, as shown in the photo. Join these pieces together in rows, working from left to right and top to bottom. Press the seams open.

⑥ Before you join the stars to one another, add border strips to the top and bottom of each block. Measure the length of the dark star and cut 2 strips of light fabric 1½ inches wide to this measurement. Follow the same steps to add dark strips to the top and bottom of the light stars. Join the three stars with the dark one in the middle, as shown on the opposite page.

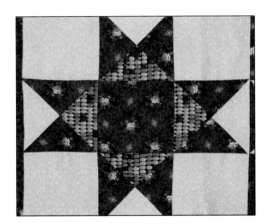

HOURGLASS BORDER

1 For the hourglass border at the ends of the piece, cut four squares of light and four squares of midtone fabric 3¼ × 3¼ inches. Following the instructions in this chapter, make eight hourglass units of light and midtone fabric. Press all seams to one side.

2 Join the hourglass units to one another. I sewed mine with the light fabric portions of each unit together, but you could choose to alternate the direction of the units as described earlier in this chapter. Experiment before you sew to see which you prefer. Following the instructions for sashing without posts in Chapter 11, add sashing 1½ inches wide to all four sides of your completed hourglass units. When complete, add a row of hourglass units to each end of the table runner.

3 Join your hourglass units to each end of your three Ohio Star blocks. Press seams open. Bind your tablerunner following instructions in Chapter 18. In this project, the midtone fabric was used for the binding. The finished size of this project is 14 × 45 inches.

Double Half-Square Triangles (Flying Geese Unit)

I have several methods for sewing these units but my favorite is the one shown here. Why? Because it's made entirely of squares and rectangles.

This basic unit of two small triangles attached to the sides of a larger triangle is most often referred to as a *Flying Geese unit* after the popular pattern of the same name.

Cut Squares and Rectangle

1. A Flying Geese unit begins with two fabrics with good contrast. Start with the rectangle piece. It must be cut to the size of a finished unit you desire (or called for in a quilt pattern) plus the normal seam allowance for a rectangle, ¼ inch on all four sides. In this example, you want to end up with a 6 × 3-inch unit, so cut a rectangle 6½ × 3½ inches. Cut two squares to the size of the rectangle's width. In this case, cut two squares 3½ × 3½ inches.

   Note: *When you cut fabric for Flying Geese units, remember that the finished size of your rectangle = the finished size of two squares. For example, if your unit has a finished size of 4 inches, the finished size of the rectangle in the unit is 4 inches and each square is 2 × 2 inches. Once you calculate the finished size of each piece of fabric, be sure to add enough for the seam allowances.*

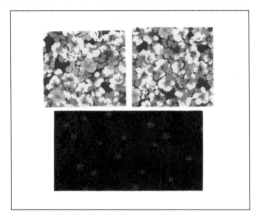

2. You are going to sew the squares to each end of the rectangle along the diagonal of the squares. When you are first practicing this technique, draw these diagonal lines on the wrong side of the squares first (a).

3. Lay one square on one end of the rectangle. Following the diagonal line you drew, sew the square to the rectangle (b).

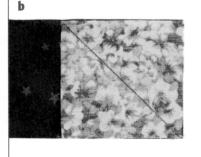

④ Lay your cutting ruler ¼ inch to the outside of the seam you just made and cut away the excess fabric. Flip the unit open. Press the seam to one side, toward the darker fabric.

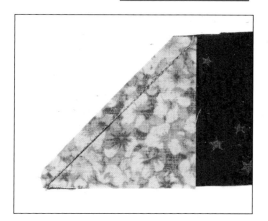

⑤ Lay your second square on the other end of the rectangle. The top of the second square should overlap the top of the first square by ¼ inch. Following the diagonal line you drew on the square, sew it to the rectangle. When the seam is finished, lay your cutting ruler ¼ inch to the outside of the seam and cut away the excess fabric. Open the unit and press the seam to one side.

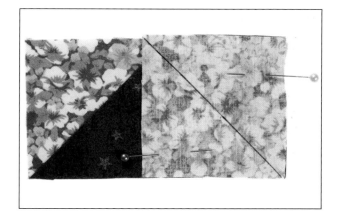

⑥ The two diagonal seams that you make when you attach your squares to the rectangle should cross one another at the top of the unit. When complete, your Flying Geese unit should have a ¼-inch seam allowance on all four sides.

 TIP

Flying Geese units are not complicated but it takes a little practice to get them to lay flat and have sufficient seam allowances on all four sides. You can use up scrap fabric with this block, so cut some pieces of light and dark fabrics to practice this technique.

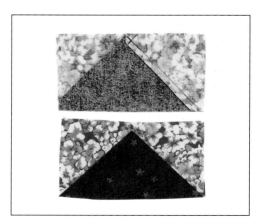

Flying Geese Quilt

As you saw with half-square and quarter-square triangles, Flying Geese units (also called double half-square triangles) can be combined with other quilting elements to create new patterns. This quilt uses Flying Geese units in two sizes. For the fabrics I combined a bright stripe with two batiks in blue and green.

MAKE A FLYING GEESE QUILT

1 For this quilt, you will need ½ yard of a bright fabric for the large Flying Geese blocks and binding, 1 yard each of a dark blue and a light blue fabric, and ½ yard of a dark green. The large Flying Geese units in this quilt are combined with rectangles then sewn together in a pattern that goes by several names, including Whirlwind, Cyclone, and Four Directions.

To make the large Flying Geese units, cut 16 rectangles from your bright fabric and your light blue fabric 8½ × 4½ inches. If you are using a striped fabric, be sure the stripes in your rectangles are all in the same direction. Cut 32 squares of dark blue, 4½ × 4½ inches. Following instructions in the previous section, make 16 Flying Geese units from your bright rectangles and dark blue squares. Sew each Flying Geese unit to a light blue rectangle in the configuration shown in the photograph.

2 Sew the large Flying Geese units to one another in sets of four so that each one is pointed in a different direction, as shown.

3 Following instructions in Chapter 12 for adding sashing around blocks, join these Cyclone units to one another with dark green sashing. All sashing and borders in this project are cut 1½ inches wide.

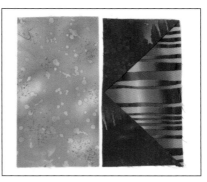

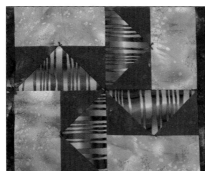

FLYING GEESE BORDER

1 Sixteen Flying Geese units are in each side border in this quilt. From the dark blue fabric, cut 32 rectangles 4½ × 2½ inches. From the light blue fabric, cut 64 squares 2½ × 2½ inches. Following the instructions to make Flying Geese units on page 178, make 32 Flying Geese units. Sew them together in eight sets of four units each. All of the Flying Geese units in each set of four should be pointing in the same direction.

2 Cut six rectangles from the dark blue, 4½ × 1½ inches. To make the Flying Geese border for the sides of the quilt, sew the 4-piece Flying Geese units and the rectangles together in this order: rectangle, Flying Geese unit pointed right, Flying Geese unit pointed left, rectangle, Flying Geese unit pointed right, Flying Geese unit pointed left, rectangle. When complete, attach one of these borders to the left and right sides of your quilt.

3 To finish, add a border of light blue to the top and bottom of your quilt following instructions in Chapter 11. Add a border of dark green to all four sides of your quilt. All single fabric borders and sashing in this project are cut 1½ inches wide. If you use a striped fabric for your binding, like the quilt pictured here, I recommend you cut it on the bias as instructed in Chapter 18. The finished size of this quilt is 38 × 44 inches. It is backed by a cotton print fabric that does not appear in the top and includes a low-loft polyester batting. It was tied (see Chapter 17).

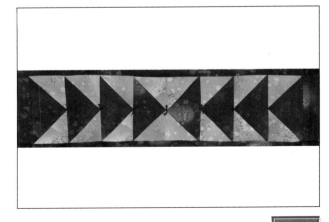

Joining Blocks Diagonally: Setting on Point

So far in your exploration of quilting, you've joined quilt blocks in horizontal rows—a method of putting a quilt together that is called a *straight set.*

But you can also join blocks to one another across the diagonal dimension of a quilt. This method is called *setting on point* or a *diagonal set,* and it's made possible by using some of the techniques learned in the previous chapter about triangles.

Straight Sets versus Setting on Point

Setting a quilt on point can make an otherwise ordinary quilt top into something far more dynamic visually, because the eye automatically associates movement with shapes that seem off balance or tipped. To illustrate this principle, I'll compare these two samples of the same quilt, one in a straight set and the other set on point. Blocks made of strips of fabric, such as the green and purple blocks below, are also called Roman Road blocks.

Method Comparison

STRAIGHT SET

This figure is an example of quilt blocks in a straight set. The sample shows a combination of small Fence Rail blocks made of three fabrics and half-square triangles made of two lighter fabrics. As you learned in Chapter 9, Fence Rail blocks are made of strips of cloth sewn to one another. When they are set like this—all in the same direction—the horizontal nature of the block is emphasized. The darker colors in the Fence Rails enhance the effect. You almost don't notice how the two lighter colors used in the half-square triangles combine to make a striped effect moving diagonally across this sample.

HORIZONTAL TO DIAGONAL

Most quilt blocks are constructed so that their opposite sides lie horizontal and vertical to the viewer, like the quilt sample above and the square of fabric on the right in this photograph. But even a simple square can be turned 45 degrees so that it appears to balance on one of its corners, like the square on the left. This tip or tilt draws your attention because the eye senses the potential for movement in the quilt.

The most common shape associated with this configuration is the diamond. When quilt blocks are sewed so that they are joined in this relationship to one another, it's called setting on point. What happens when you set a lot of quilt blocks on point?

SETTING ON POINT

This quilt uses exactly the same combination of fabrics and blocks as the straight set sample on the preceding page but look at the difference a setting makes. Now the Fence Rail blocks are tipped up on their points and the seams which join the two pieces of the half-square triangles draw the eye to the vertical lines created by matching the colors between rows. Now the Fence Rails function like units of color enhanced by the spring hues of the half-square triangles. This floating sensation is emphasized by the dark-green border and binding of the same fabric in a color that recedes (see photograph of the entire quilt on the next page).

This design now has movement. The eye hops from one Fence Rail block to another instead of moving only from left to right as it did in the first sample. The subtle vertical paths created by the half-square triangles provide places for the eye to rest

DIAGONAL TAKES UP MORE SPACE

One other factor that a quilter may consider when making a decision about how to set a quilt is size. Notice the difference in size between these blocks. The blocks sitting horizontally are 3½ inches across. When measured across the diagonal, these same blocks are 4¾ inches across. The quilt project in this chapter, which begins on the following page, is six blocks across. If they were straight set, this would give you a quilt top width of 18 inches. Set on point, the same six blocks make a row that's 24 inches wide.

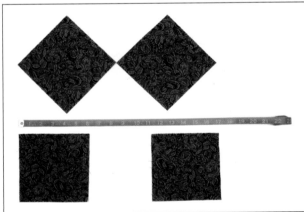

Garden of Violets Lap Quilt Overview

For me, one of the first signs of spring is the deep purples and blues of violets that bloom in my gardens. Set among their dark green leaves, these diminutive flowers herald the return of color to my New England yard. The colors of this quilt were inspired by this annual display.

WHAT YOU NEED TO KNOW

For this project, you need to know how to:

Rotary cut and sew quarter- and half-square triangles. (See Chapter 13.)

Cut and sew strip sets. (See Chapter 9.)

Add a border to a quilt top. (See Chapter 11.)

WHAT YOU WILL LEARN

In this project, you will learn how to:

Construct a quilt by sewing rows together diagonally.

Make a floating border.

Cut and sew setting and corner triangles to a quilt top.

Materials

TOP

Fence Rail (Roman Road) Blocks

6 fat quarters in your chosen color scheme (I used three purple and three green fat quarters)

Half-Square Triangles

½ yard each of two fabrics in lighter hues of the fabrics chosen for the Fence Rail blocks

BORDER, BINDING, BACKING

2 yards of dark fabric to complement the quilt top's blocks (In this quilt, the border fabric is also included in some of the Fence Rail blocks.)

BATTING

Medium loft polyester, 44 × 60 inches

I tied this quilt using different hues of perle cotton in purple and green.

Garden of Violets lap quilt. Finished size: 32 × 50 inches.

Garden of Violets Block Construction

The details of making a Fence Rail block are covered in depth in Chapter 9. You need 45 Fence Rail blocks for this quilt. Full instructions for half-square triangles can be found in Chapter 13. Review those instructions for more information if needed.

Cut and Sew Blocks

FENCE RAIL BLOCKS

1. Even the edges of each of your fat quarters. Cut five strips from each fabric, 1½ inches wide, for a total of 30 strips of cloth (a).

2. Combine the strips in assorted ways in sets of three and sew them together in strip sets. (I made one strip set of purple and one of green; the rest of the sets combine both colors.) You will have 10 strip sets total. Press seams to one side. Cut five blocks from each strip set, 3½ inches long (b), for a total of 50 blocks.

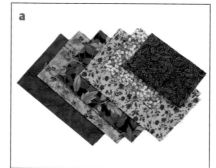

HALF-SQUARE TRIANGLE BLOCKS

3. Cut three strips of fabric from each of your two light fabrics, 3⅞ inches wide. Following the instructions in Chapter 13 for half-square triangles, make 60 units of two colors for this quilt.

All quilt top construction benefits from careful layout prior to sewing blocks and rows together, but this is even truer for a quilt set on point. Like a straight set, the rows in this quilt are sewn together with straight seams in straight rows. But the thrust of the pattern is diagonal.

① This layout is easiest to see if you begin by laying out the blocks that are consistent throughout the quilt. In this case, that is the half-square triangles. Set them out in ten rows of 6 squares each, working from top to bottom. As you place the units next to one another, their corners should just touch. Turn the half-square triangles so that the same colors are adjacent to one another.

② Once you've laid out your half-square triangles, place your Fence Rail blocks in the spaces among them. Do not put Fence Rail blocks around the outside perimeter of the top. Turn the Fence Rails so that their seams are all moving in the same direction. Once you've laid out the entire quilt top, step back to view the overall impact of the Fence Rail blocks. Do you have too much purple in one area? Too much green? Adjust them until you are happy.

Now that you have the blocks laid out, the difference between a straight set quilt and one set on point becomes apparent!

What do you do about the triangular spaces open on the sides (see photo)? You fill them with *setting triangles.* Setting triangles are quarter-square triangles (see Chapter 13) and we could cut them using the same math. But most quilters like to cut their setting triangles even larger so they have more fabric around the outside of a quilt top. You make them big at first and then cut them down to size later. Here's how.

1 Count the number of setting triangles needed to fill the spaces on the top, bottom, and sides of your quilt. Do not include the triangles needed in the four corners. Divide the number of triangles by 4 (the number of quarter-square triangles in a square of fabric). For this quilt, you need 28 setting triangles. Divided by 4, this means you need to cut seven squares of fabric. If your division does not come out even, round up to the next highest number.

2 Measure one of the blocks in your quilt top on the diagonal. Add 2 inches to this measurement. Cut your setting triangle squares to this size. In the example, the quilt blocks are 4 inches across the diagonal so you need to cut seven squares 6 × 6 inches. Once your setting triangles are cut, lay them in place around the outside of your quilt layout.

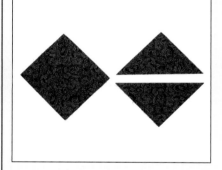

3 The four corners of the quilt top will be squared up with *corner triangles.* Cut two squares the size of your block plus 1½ inches. For this quilt, that is 4 inches for the block plus 1½ inches for a total of 5½ inches. Cut these two squares in half diagonally. Place one of these half-square triangles in each corner so that you can see what the whole quilt top will look like.

Sewing a quilt top on the diagonal takes some focused attention because you have to think in straight and diagonal lines at the same time. If you can, plan for a block of time long enough to put the whole quilt top together at once.

Lay out Quilt Blocks

1 If you were to try to sew these blocks to one another from left to right, as you have in the projects in previous chapters, your seams would have to zigzag up and down in order to attach the blocks to one another. Inevitably, you would end up attaching one block to two others simultaneously. This sort of seam is called a *set-in seam*. They can be a challenge to sew well because it is difficult to handle the fabric in the corners. But what if you change the way you sew your blocks together?

2 If you look at these blocks on the diagonal you can easily see how they can be joined in straight rows. That's the trick in understanding how to sew a quilt top on point—you find the way to sew the blocks to one another in a straight line because making this type of seam is much easier to negotiate.

3 I recommend sewing the blocks of each individual row together without their setting triangles. Do not sew the rows to one another until you lay them out again to make sure every block is in the right place and going in the right direction. Corrections are much easier to make at this stage than later on. I sew my blocks together one at a time. Before I pick up the next block, I lay the ones that are joined back in their place in the quilt top in order to double-check direction and placement.

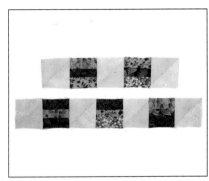

CONTINUED ON NEXT PAGE

Add Setting Triangles

1 Once the blocks of each row are sewn together, add a setting triangle to the end of each row. Lay them out before you do this. The longest edge (*hypotenuse*) of each triangle is kept to the outside of each row. Align the 90-degree angle of each triangle with the corner of the quilt block to which it will be attached. If you do the layout first, this will be very apparent. Just remember to keep the longest side of each triangle to the outside of the quilt top. Because of their size, the triangles will overlap.

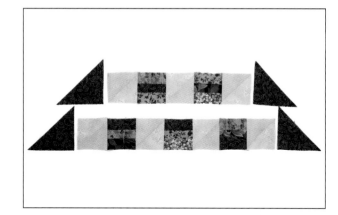

2 Sew a setting triangle to both ends of each row in your quilt top. Note that the beginning and ending rows are each composed of a single quilt block with a triangle on either side. Press the seams toward the quilt blocks, not toward the setting triangles.

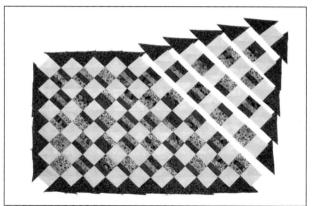

TIP

I recommend sewing the rows together in groups and then sew the groups together. For example, 15 rows are in this quilt. I sewed them together in three groups of five rows each and then joined the groups. This method minimizes the number of times the first rows are handled, lessening the chance of fraying or stretching. Also, quilt tops become heavy as they grow and this way, the full weight of the quilt top is managed only once. For full instructions on sewing rows together, please see the next page.

Sew Rows Together

1 Because of their size, the setting triangles will overlap one another when the rows are sewn together. Note in the first picture that the top row is shorter than the one on the bottom (a). In the second picture, the shorter row has been turned over so that the rows are right sides facing. Note the place where the setting triangles cross one another (b). This crossing will be sewn as part of the seam joining the rows together.

2 To ensure that the points of the triangles match when two rows are sewn together, insert a pin into the triangle point of the row on the top (a). Push the pin through the fabric of the first row. Hold the two rows apart a little so you can see where the triangle point is in the second row. Insert the pin point into this spot (b). This action automatically aligns the points in the half-square triangles in both rows simultaneously.

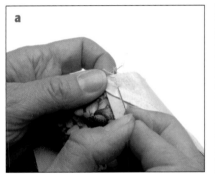

TIP

To minimize bulk, press the seams of the rows open.

Create a Floating Border

When setting and corner triangles are cut from the same fabric (usually dark) and used as the border on a quilt, the result is referred to as a *floating border*. This sameness of color works, like so many other parts of quilting, by means of the contrast between dark and light fabrics. In this quilt-top example, the contrast between the dark green on the outside of the quilt and the half-square triangles made of light colors is enough to make the center of the quilt top float visually.

Trim Triangles

1 Because the corner and setting triangles are cut big for this quilt, they make a wide seam allowance around the perimeter of the project. If you wish, you can trim this allowance down to ¼ to ½ inch before you add a border of another fabric or skip the border entirely and bind the quilt following instructions in Chapter 18. Before you add any border, trim the outside edges so they are even all around. In this example, it was trimmed to 1 inch all around the quilt.

2 Following the instructions in Chapter 11, measure the quilt top's length and cut or piece strips to this length, 3½ inches wide. Sew one border strip to each side of the quilt. Press the seams open. Measure the quilt's width. Cut two strips to this length from your border fabric, 3½ inches wide. Join them to the top and bottom of the quilt. Press the seams open.

③ The color of a floating border must be of the same fabric on all four sides of a quilt's top. Complete this pool of color by binding your quilt with the same fabric as the border. See Chapter 18 for binding instructions.

chapter 15

Crazy Quilting and String Piecing

After all the precision required for cutting and sewing triangles or setting a quilt top on point, have fun and experiment with a looser style known as crazy quilting and its near relative, string piecing. For those of you who are completely new to quilting or want a way to gain some confidence with color, crazy quilting gives you a chance to practice your sewing skills and play with all those terrific fabrics in your stash.

Two different ways to crazy quilt are explained in this chapter. The first, commonly called *sew and flip,* makes use of your scrap fabric. The second, called *stack and slash,* is perfect for fat quarters.

Traditionally, a Log Cabin block begins with a small piece of fabric at its center around which other pieces of fabric are added in successively larger sizes. This idea of building around a center is the key to creating Crazy Quilt blocks. You'll begin this chapter with a quick overview of a traditional Log Cabin block, then apply this knowledge to a crazy quilting process known as *sew and flip*.

Log Cabin Block Construction

1. Traditional Log Cabin blocks begin with a center, usually of red fabric to represent the hearth of a home (a). This piece of fabric is 2½ inches square.

2. In a Log Cabin block, half of the logs are of light fabric, half of dark. A piece of light fabric of the same size (2½ inches square) is joined to the center piece (b).

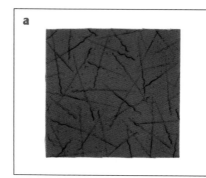
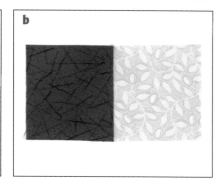

3. In Log Cabin, every new log is cut to the size needed to cover the raw edges of the side to which it is being attached. In this example, two 2½-inch squares of fabric are stitched together for a total of 4½ inches (4 inches true size plus a ½-inch seam allowance). In order to cover the raw edges of one side of these two squares, you need a piece of fabric that's 4½ inches long. (All logs in this example are cut 2½ inches wide.)

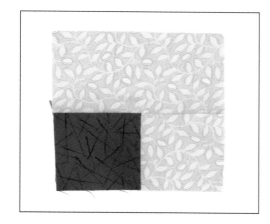

④ The next log in this block covers the same length as the one before, 4½ inches. Before you move to the next step, notice what has happened to the measurement at the bottom of this growing block. It includes your original center block, its same-size mate, as well as the width of the log you just added. The total length of the raw edge at the bottom of this block is now 6½ inches. The next two logs added to this block will be 6½ inches long.

Also note that the logs are added to the growing block in this sequence—dark, dark, light, light.

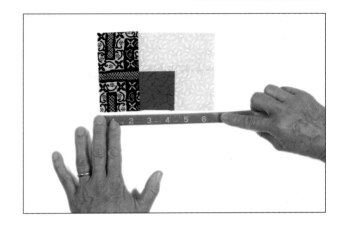

⑤ Once the two 6½-inch logs are added, your growing square has a raw edge at the top totaling 8½ inches. This idea of adding logs long enough to cover the raw edges of each side of the growing block is the key idea you need to understand when you create Crazy Quilt blocks on a sewing machine or by hand.

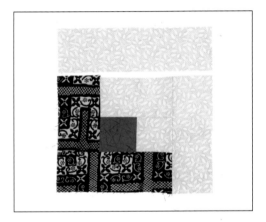

⑥ The two blocks pictured here show how successively larger pieces of fabric in light and dark colors combine to create an exciting visual pattern that allows a quilter to play with color. Next you will apply the Log Cabin technique to crazy quilting.

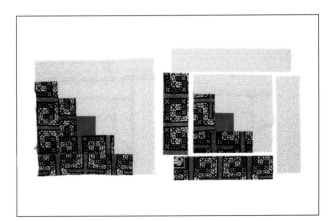

Create a Crazy Quilt Block

In crazy quilting, small pieces of irregularly shaped fabric are stitched to a *foundation*, a sturdy piece of cloth that holds all of the pieces together. The resulting block functions almost like a new piece of fabric. It can be cut and resewn into all sorts of shapes. This type of quilting is adventurous, because you're never quite sure where it will end up.

CHOOSE A FOUNDATION FABRIC

1 When you build a house, you start with a good foundation, something sturdy that will hold the entire structure in place. Crazy quilting begins with the same principle. Because you are going to use several small scraps of fabric to create your block, you need to sew them to a fabric that won't stretch or fray. In crazy quilting, the most common foundation fabric is unbleached muslin. It's relatively inexpensive, it's stable, and every fabric store carries bolts of it.

2 Crazy quilt squares begin with a square of muslin cut 2 inches larger than the size of the block you want in the end. In other words, if you want 10-inch blocks, start with muslin that is cut 12 inches square. As you sew scraps of fabric to the muslin, the various seams each take up a bit of cloth so you lose a little bit of dimension. The extra 2 inches makes up for this plus a little extra.

As a general guide, a yard of muslin yields nine 12-inch squares, 20 8-inch squares or 36 6-inch squares.

Since crazy quilt squares are made of scrap, you don't have to measure fabric precisely as you do when you piece a block for a patchwork quilt. The size of each scrap is determined by the length of the raw edges it needs to cover.

CHOOSE COLORS

Your next decision concerns color. You can, of course, use any scrap of fabric in a crazy quilt square if you like. Many people do. But if you want a particular result—summer colors or something predominately blue, for example—then you have to choose your scraps accordingly. This example uses a predominance of cool colors—blue, green, and purple—for the quilt block. Whatever your choice, sort your scraps to fit your criteria, and press them flat.

SEW AND FLIP

1 You start your Crazy Quilt block in the center of your piece of muslin just like you start piecing a traditional Log Cabin block with the center fabric. Choose two scraps of approximately the same size (a).

2 Lay one scrap in the center of your muslin, right side up. Lay the second scrap of fabric wrong side up on top of it, aligning two edges that are approximately the same length (b). Don't worry about cutting to fit, similar lengths will do.

3 The sewing process of crazy quilting is called *sew and flip.* For the sew part, choose the edges that are approximately the same length and stitch them to the muslin. Don't bother to pin. These are short seams and the fabric will stay in place.

CONTINUED ON NEXT PAGE

④ Next is the flip part of sew and flip. After you clip the threads and remove the block from the machine, flip the fabric that's wrong side up to right side up. Press it flat in this position.

⑤ Remember the Log Cabin principle (discussed in the previous section of this chapter) that every new log had to cover all the raw edges on one side of the block? The same holds true in crazy quilting. For your third scrap, choose a piece of fabric that's long enough to cover the combined length of the raw edges on one side of your first two scraps.

⑥ Turn your third scrap wrong side up and align one of its edges along the top of your first two scraps. Sew this scrap into place, clip the threads, remove it from the machine, flip the newest scrap right side up, and press it flat.

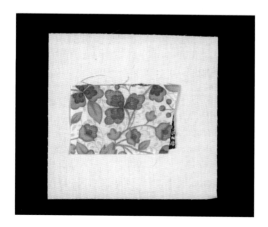

7 Working around the center pieces, add scraps of fabric to your block. Remember to always choose scraps large enough to cover all of the raw edges of the side to which it is being attached.

8 When you get to the outside edge of your muslin square, don't bother to cut your scraps to fit before you sew them. Let them spill over the edge of the muslin. Once your muslin square is completely covered, turn it over and rotary cut around its edges to even the scraps with the muslin. After you cut away the excess scrap fabric, measure your square then cut it to fit your requirements. Remember to include seam allowances in your calculations!

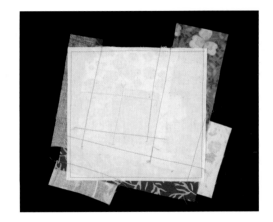

9 Once you cut your square to size, take the time to stitch around its outside edge. Sew as close to the outside edge as you can so that this stitching will not show when you join the individual blocks together. This stitching keeps the edges of the scraps from stretching or fraying as you work with the blocks.

Note: *You can stitch several smaller scraps together to create a larger piece to use in your Crazy Quilt block. As you stitch the pieces together, keep their top edges aligned. Press the seams of these combined pieces open to reduce bulk then randomly even off the bottom of the piece—either straight across or at an angle—before adding it to your block.*

Create a
String-Pieced Block

When you true the edge of a piece of fabric, as explained in Chapter 5, you create what's known in quilting as a *string*. Years ago, quilters joined these long, narrow strips together to make blocks for their quilts. *String piecing*, as this process is called, can be done without a foundation (see the Stack of Coins pattern in Chapter 11). But string piecing with a foundation—a process similar to the sew-and-flip construction method described in the previous section—provides more flexibility.

String Piece with a Foundation

1 Begin with unbleached muslin cut at least an inch wider than the final size of the desired square/rectangle.

2 Sort strings for size/color. Include only strings long enough to cover the foundation piece. Strings less than 1 inch wide are not a good choice—they add bulk to the finished piece without adding much color. You can cut strings from larger pieces of fabric. If you cut new strings, they do not need to be the same width.

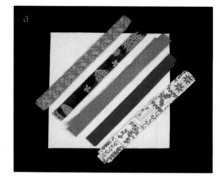 

3 String piecing begins at the bottom of your foundation piece. With the right side up, align the bottom edge of your first string with the bottom edge of your foundation. Stitch the top of the string to the foundation with a ¼-inch seam.

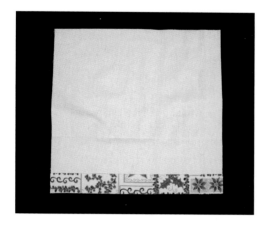

4 Lay your second string, wrong side up, on top of your first. Align the top edge of this string with the seamed edge of your first piece. Sew your second string to the foundation along this edge. Flip it over as you would in the sew-and-flip process of crazy quilting and press.

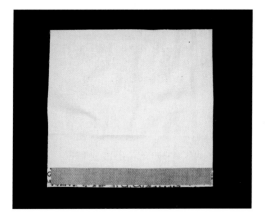

5 Continue adding strings to your block. Unlike patchwork, strings do not have to be the same width nor do their sides need to be parallel to one another. In fact, the block will be more interesting if they are not.

Note: Typically, strings from your scrap bag will not have parallel sides, and these are fine for string piecing. One caution, however, as you build your block. If you add a string with a narrow end on the left and a wide end on the right, add your next irregular string in the opposite way—wide end on the left and narrow end on the right. This technique maintains a balance in the overall block even though individual strings may look as though they tip to one side or the other.

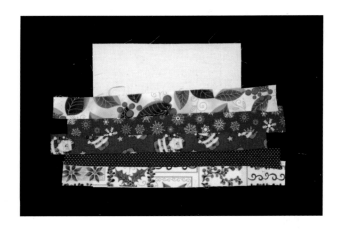

6 Once you have covered your foundation with strings, turn it wrong side up and rotary cut any excess fabric to even the strings with your foundation piece. Turn it over to the right side and stitch the loose raw edges at the top and bottom of the block to the foundation.

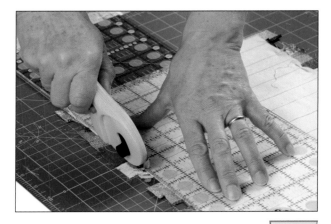

A second method to create Crazy Quilt blocks begins with new fabric, not scraps. The method is called *stack and slash* because you stack squares of fabric in a pile, cut them (slash) at odd angles then sew the various pieces together. A number of variations of this method exist, but this is the basic technique.

1 Stack and slash begins with squares of six different fabrics. Choose fabrics as you would for a patchwork project, united around a common theme or color scheme in a variety of print sizes and contrasts. In these squares, there are three prints with Asian motifs (often referred to as Orientals in quilting), a fourth print with strong colors in an abstract design, a fifth print with brighter colors and a large botanical print, and a neutral fabric in an oversized floral.

2 Determine what size you want in your complete square, add a half inch to that size for seam allowances then add another 3 inches to that to allow for the fabric that you lose in multiple seams during the stack-and-slash process. For this example, you want a finished size of 5 inches so begin by cutting 8½-inch squares of each fabric.

3 As you build stack-and-slash squares, keep your squares in order or the process doesn't work. Cut or tear six small pieces of paper, number them 1 through 6 and pin them to the upper left-hand corner of the fabric squares. Pile your fabric squares on top of one another in numerical order, with 1 on the top and 6 on the bottom, aligning the edges. This is the stack of stack and slash.

4 Place your pile of squares in the center of your cutting mat and lay your cutting ruler across the squares at a random angle (a).

Note: Experience has taught me to keep this angle at least an inch away from any of the four corners.

5 Take your rotary cutter, hold the ruler firmly, and cut across the pile of squares through all six fabrics (b). This is the slash part of stack and slash.

6 Now this is the key step. Do not touch the numbered pile of fabric. This pile remains in exactly the same order throughout this process. But take the bottom piece of fabric from the unnumbered pile and bring it to the top of this same pile. Go through the pile of squares, one at a time, and join the two pieces to each other. You end up with six squares, half of one fabric, half of another. Press the seams open to reduce bulk.

CONTINUED ON NEXT PAGE

7 Pile the squares back in order, with number 1 on top and number 6 on the bottom. Align the edges as best you can. This aligning gets more difficult as the process continues because of the pinned numbers and the seams. You won't be able to be exact. Just align the squares as best you can. Once they are aligned, lay your cutting ruler across the pile at a different random angle and cut through the pile with your rotary cutter.

8 Do not move the fabric in the numbered pile. This time, take the two bottom pieces from the unnumbered pile and move them to the top of the same pile. Go through the pile and sew the new pairs together. Press the seams open.

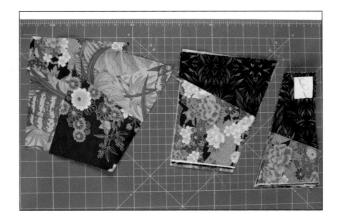

9 Pile the squares back in order, with number 1 on top and number 6 on the bottom. Align the edges as best you can. You're going to slash the pile of squares for a third and last time but before you do, take some time to lay your cutting ruler across the pile in different directions to see what kind of a cut might make the most interesting design. For example, if your first two cuts are from side to side, your squares might benefit from an angled cut from top to bottom. Once you make this decision, slash your pile of squares. Take care that the pins attaching the numbered papers to the fabric are not in the way of your rotary cutter.

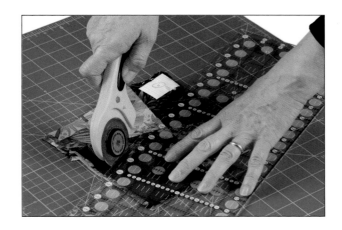

10 Do not move the fabric in the numbered pile. This time, take the three bottom pieces from the unnumbered pile and move them to the top of the same pile. You can go through the pile again, sewing these new pairs together. But when you get to this stage, you should instead lay out the six pairs (after you move the bottom three from the unnumbered pile) so that you can see the complete squares before you sew. Do this to make sure you won't have the same fabrics butting up to one another in the new seam and to make sure you've got the most interesting combinations possible. Once satisfied, sew the new pairs together and press the seams open.

11 When you complete Step 10, you have squares that truly deserve the name "crazy," as you can see in this photograph. These very uneven blocks are caused by the fabric shifting while you cut and by sewing the fabric at odd angles. To even them up, start by locating a corner or edge that seems the straightest to you. Align that with a measuring line on your cutting mat. Lay your ruler down and even one side of the square, taking off the least amount of fabric you can. Do this to all four sides and all six squares. Do not attempt to cut the squares to size as you even the sides.

12 Once your sides are even, measure the squares one at a time. You are looking for the shortest dimension of all, which should be close to your finished size. Cut all of the squares to your finished size or to match the smallest dimension.

Crazy Quilt a Handbag

This is a project you can make in an afternoon using either crazy quilt or string-pieced squares. There's no quilting, tying or batting involved. These fun bags are fully lined and the extra long strap allows you to sling it across your shoulders so it is comfortable to carry.

WHAT YOU NEED TO KNOW

For this project, you need to know:

How to cut fabric with a rotary cutter and sew a straight seam (chapters 5 and 6).

WHAT YOU WILL LEARN

In this project, you will learn how to:

Combine crazy quilt or string pieced squares with other fabrics to create new fabric combinations.

Materials

BAG EXTERIOR

6 squares of muslin measuring 6½ × 6½ inches

6 squares of fabric in color or pattern to complement crazy quilt or string-pieced squares measuring 6½ × 8 inches. A fat quarter is perfect for this.

Scraps of cotton, brocade, silk, or velvet in sufficient quantity to cover muslin

LINING AND STRAP

½ yard

① Following the instructions for crazy quilt or string-pieced squares in this chapter, cut and sew four squares that will end up measuring 6½ × 8 inches. From your alternate fabric, cut 4 rectangles measuring 6½ × 8 inches. Sew them together in two rows, alternating the types of squares. The top row begins with a crazy quilt square followed by an alternate square. The second row begins with an alternate square followed by a crazy quilt square. Join the two rows to one another. This is your bag's exterior.

② Cut a rectangle 15 × 24 inches from your lining fabric. Set this piece aside for the bag's lining.

Cut strips from your lining fabric 4 inches wide and the equivalent of 40 inches long. If you need to piece fabric to make the strap long enough, be sure to add seam allowances into your calculations. Fold the strap in half lengthwise, wrong side out and sew it along its length. When you are done, clip a safety pin to the side of one of the strap's open ends.

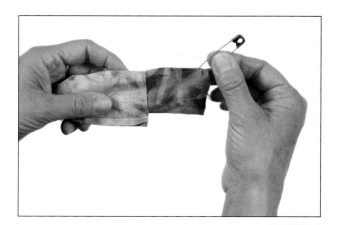

③ Push the safety pin's closed end into the tube you have sewn for your strap. Maneuver the pin further and further into the tube with your fingers until it emerges at the opposite open end of the tube. Grasp the pin and keep pulling until you have turned the tube inside out. When this process is complete, press the right-side-out tube flat.

CONTINUED ON NEXT PAGE

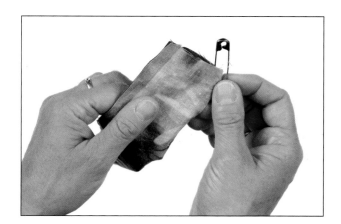

4 Examine the bag exterior you sewed of crazy quilt and alternate squares. Working from left to right, notice there are three seams. Working at the top edge, center and pin the open ends of the strap to the first and third seams. The bulk of the strap should be hanging in the opposite direction of these open ends. Be sure the strap is not twisted.

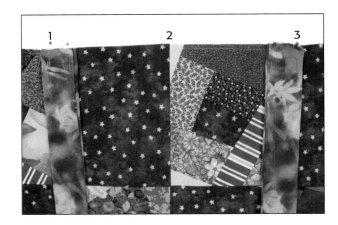

5 Lay the lining on the exterior, right sides together. Pin them together along their top edges, including the open ends of the strap. Sew the exterior of the bag, its lining, and the strap together.

6 Once this seam is complete, unfold the whole bag right side up and lay it out in front of you with the lining on your left. Now fold the bag in half from top to bottom. Align the two ends of the seam you made in the previous step and pin these two edges together. Make sure the strap is not caught in your pins. Now stitch this seam. When you are done, you will have a large tube with the strap on the inside.

⑦ Turn the bag so that the open end of the exterior is at the top. Pick it up by the seams at the two top corners. Now move your hands toward one another, letting the bag come open. Keep moving your hands until the two corners you are holding touch one another. As you do this, the two seams to which the strap is attached become the new outside corners of the bag. This movement ensures that the bag's strap will be in the correct place when the bag is complete.

Pin the open end of the bag's exterior closed, aligning seams where they meet. Sew the end of the bag's exterior closed. Make sure the strap does not get caught in your stitching. Turn the bag right side out.

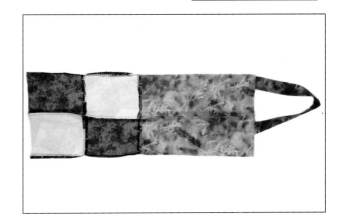

⑧ Reach inside the bag and press your fingers into its corners to push them out as far as they can go. Now hold the bag up by the open end of its lining. Turn the raw edges of the lining in ¼ inch; pin then stitch this opening closed. Once this seam is complete, use your fingers to push the lining into the bag's exterior. Again, push the corners out as far as they can go.

⑨ Press the entire bag, making sure the open end is flat. You might add a row of stitches around the open end close to the edge to keep the exterior and lining in place.

TIP

To make a custom-fit strap, measure the length from just below the left side of your waist, over your right shoulder and back to your starting point. Cut your strap fabric to this length. Your bag will comfortably ride at your hip with the strap over the opposite shoulder. This positioning relieves stress on your shoulders and neck while leaving your hands free.

Stack-and-Slash Lap Quilt

This dramatic lap quilt uses six blocks created by the stack-and-slash method described earlier in this chapter. Surrounded (that is, backed and bound) by black fabric and accented with strips of color, this warmer catches the eye.

This lap quilt is hand quilted using the stitch-in-a-ditch method, as described in Chapter 17.

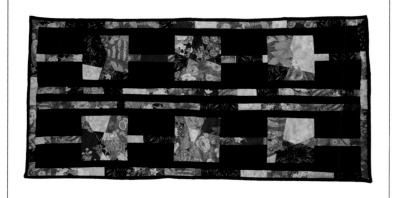

WHAT YOU NEED TO KNOW

For this project, you need to know:

How to cut fabric with a rotary cutter and sew a straight seam (chapters 5 and 6).

WHAT YOU WILL LEARN

In this project, you will learn how to:

Integrate the strip set technique in Chapter 9 with the stack and slash technique in this chapter.

Materials

TOP, BACKING, AND BINDING

½ yard each of six fabrics for stack-and-slash squares, accenting stripes, and border

1½ yards of solid black for sashing, binding, and backing

BATTING

Low-loft batting in polyester, cotton, or a blend of both that's good for hand quilting

1 Using the stack-and-slash instructions from earlier in this chapter, make six blocks with colors of your choice. Even them up to 6-in. squares. Cut two strips the full length of your fabric from each of the six fabrics used in the blocks, 1 inch wide. If you used fat quarters to make your blocks, cut three strips.

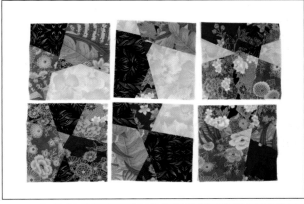

2 Cut the 1-inch strips to various lengths between 2 and 4 inches. Join them randomly end to end until you have strips that measure at least 40 inches. Don't make them too much longer than this because they will become unwieldy.

3 Cut four strips of black fabric 3 inches wide and as long as your fabric is wide. In other words, cut them from selvedge to selvedge along the crossgrain. Remove the selvedges. Make two strip sets in this configuration: black, colorful pieced strip, black.

CONTINUED ON NEXT PAGE

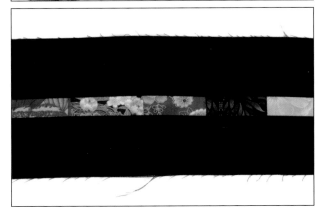

④ Once the strip sets are complete, cut eight squares 6 × 6 inches from them.

⑤ Lay your stack-and-slash squares and strip-set squares out in two rows of seven blocks each in this order: strip-set square, stack-and-slash square. Each row should begin and end with a strip-set square. Join these squares together in two rows, and press the seams open. Measure the lengths of these two rows to make sure they are the same. If not, then trim them to the same length.

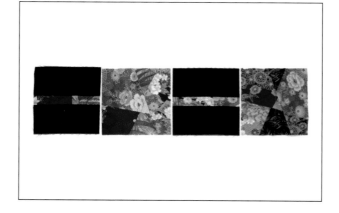

⑥ Cut five strips of black fabric 1½ inches wide along the crossgrain. Remove their selvedges. Create a strip set in this order: black strip, pieced-color strip, black strip, pieced-color strip, black strip. Press the seams toward the black fabric. Cut this strip set to the same length as the rows created in Step 5.

7 The following set of photographs will guide you in putting this quilt top together in the proper order. Sew a row of squares to each side of the strip set you made in Step 6. Press the seams open to reduce bulk.

8 Add a 1½ inch-wide strip of black to both sides of the pieces you joined in Step 7. When you complete this step, measure the length of the piece down the middle. Cut two borders from your color strips to this length. If you don't have a color strip long enough, join the pieces you do have until you attain the correct length.

9 Sew the colorful pieced border strips to each side of the quilt top. Press the seams toward the black fabric. Measure the top from side to side across the middle. Cut two border pieces made of strips to this length and add them to the top and bottom of the quilt top. Bind the quilt with black fabric following instructions in Chapter 18.

chapter 16

Backing, Batting, and Basting

Once your quilt top is complete, then it's time to make the quilt sandwich. You do this by making a backing for your project, layering it with batting between the quilt top and the backing, and then basting the three layers together so they can be quilted or tied.

This chapter is about some choices that are as important as the fabrics you select for the top of your project. The basic skills required for the steps in this chapter are: truing an edge, cutting fabric with a rotary cutter, and hand sewing.

Backing

Traditionally, quilt tops were backed by unbleached muslin because it was readily available, sturdy, and agreed with every fabric in color and tone. Besides, when a quilt is on a bed, no one sees the back, right?

Muslin is still a good choice for these reasons, and quilt fabric manufacturers now make muslin in 60- to 90-inch widths, the perfect size for a large quilt. But contemporary quilters view a quilt's back as a second place to play with fabric, though to a lesser degree than the top.

SELECT FABRIC FOR BACKING

① A quilt's back functions as a stabilizing unit in a quilt. For this reason, make it out of as few pieces as possible. Many quilters watch for sales and purchase long lengths of fabric for backing. Some quilters piece backing from larger pieces of scrap often selected for a common color or print scheme. Other quilters use up extra blocks from other projects as part of their backings. Others like the traditional look of antique quilts so they choose muslin. Probably the most common choice is a backing made from one of the fabrics used in the front of the quilt. This photograph shows examples of all of these choices.

TIP

No matter what you choose to use for your quilt's backing, select the same quality fabric for your quilt's back as you did for its top. Differences in quality show up in varying shrink rates when a quilt is laundered, causing puckering. Selecting dark-colored backings for light-colored tops is also not a good idea. The darker color can cast a shadow over the front. Also, even though it may seem like a good idea, please don't use bed sheets for your quilt backings. The weave of bed linens is tighter than other fabrics, making them difficult to quilt or tie.

MEASURE FOR BACKING

2 Measure the length and width of your completed quilt top as you would for a border, which is down the middle of the top. If your quilt project is small—a place mat or table runner, for example—add 2 inches to the length and width of these measurements for your backing. If your project is larger, add 4 to 6 inches to the top, bottom, and side measurements of your quilt top for your backing.

3 Use the following table to calculate the yardage you need for your quilt project's backing. These measurements are based on fabric from 40 to 42 inches wide. Fabric manufacturers now offer a limited range of fabric in widths up to 120 inches. If you want a one-piece backing, these are a good option.

CONTINUED ON NEXT PAGE

Backing Yardage	
Quilt Width	*Length of Fabric Needed*
36 inches or less	Length of quilt project plus 4 inches
37 to 78 inches wide and less than 78 inches long	Width of the quilt (if it is 78 inches or less long) plus 4 inches × 2 (This backing requires one seam across the width of the quilt.)
37 to 78 inches wide and more than 78 inches long	Length of the quilt (if it is longer than 78 inches) plus 4 inches × 2 (This backing requires one seam down the length of the quilt.)
More than 78 inches wide and 79 to 120 inches long	Width of the quilt plus 6 inches × 3 (This backing requires two seams across the width of the quilt.)

④ Once you settle on the fabric for your quilt backing, cut it to the proper length and width plus 2 to 6 inches on all four sides. If you need to piece, follow the guidelines indicated in this illustration.

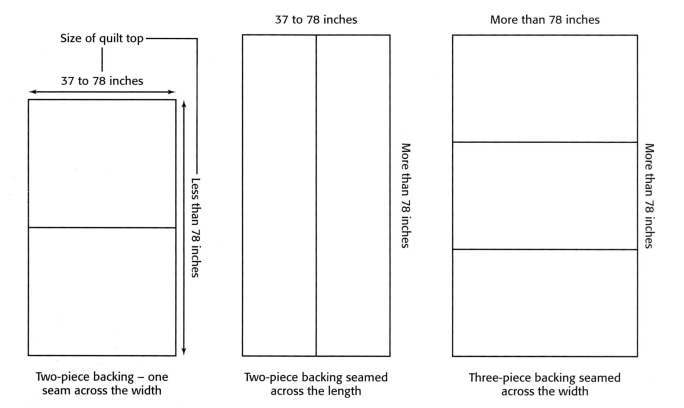

Two-piece backing – one
seam across the width

Two-piece backing seamed
across the length

Three-piece backing seamed
across the width

TIP

Press the seams of your pieced backings open for ease
of quilting.

Batting can be bought by the yard, like fabric, or rolled up in a bag. Sooner or later, most quilters find a batting that suits their style of quilting. But not all batts are created equal. This section explains some guidelines for your selection process.

Batting on rolls in quilt shop.

Batting in bags.

BATTING VOCABULARY

Bearding: When you quilt, your needle and thread can drag bits of batting through the holes the needle makes in the fabric. In general, cotton batts have a tendency to do this less than synthetic fiber batts. But manufacturers have minimized this problem by utilizing various processes that lock the fibers of a batt together (called *needle punching*) or by treating the surface of a batt with heat or chemicals to hold its fibers in place (*thermobonding* or *glazing*).

Loft: This term is commonly used when quilters refer to the thickness of a particular batt. But it also refers to the resiliency of the fibers in a batt. In general, choose a low loft (thinner) batt for hand quilting, a low to medium loft for machine quilting, and a high loft for tying if you want the visual impact of a fluffy comforter.

Needling: This refers to the relative ease or difficulty you have when pushing a needle through a given batt as you quilt. You often hear quilters say something like "It needles well," to refer to a batting that's particularly easy to quilt. This is true even if you machine quilt. As always, if you are unsure of a batt's needling, then get samples of different batts to try.

> **TIP**
>
> Don't skimp on size when you buy batting. As a general rule, add a total of 12 inches to the length and width dimensions of your quilt top to get the right sized batt for large projects, add 8 inches for medium-sized projects, and add 4 inches for small projects.

Natural versus Synthetic Fibers

Wool and then cotton were the original battings of choice. Then in the late 1960s, manufacturers started offering batts made from synthetic fibers such as polyester. This was a breakthrough because polyester fibers did not require the same close quilting to secure cotton or wool batts. You can wash a quilt filled with synthetic fibers and throw it in the dryer without fear of shrinkage or fiber breakdown. But cotton and wool batting have made a strong comeback among quilters in recent years.

CHARACTERISTICS OF COTTON BATTS

- Keep sleepers warm without trapping body heat like polyester.
- Shrink from 1 to 5 percent when laundered.
- The best choice for antique-looking quilts.
- More opaque than synthetics so dark backings are not as much of a problem.
- Some cotton battings require pre-soaking and rinsing before use.
- If you have a cotton batt and a synthetic batt of the same loft, the cotton batt will be heavier.

Photo courtesy of Mountain Mist.

TIP

If you are tying your quilt, place your ties closer together (about every 4 inches) if using cotton batting, because cotton fibers soften over time and move around inside the quilt.

CHARACTERISTICS OF WOOL BATTS

- Wool batts are beloved by many members of the quilting community for their needling ease.
- Wool batts are now mothproof.
- Treat quilts with wool batts as if they were fine wool sweaters—wash them by hand, then lay them flat on a towel-covered floor or other surface to dry.

Note: Laundering can be very controversial in quilting. Some people believe that a quilt should never be washed because it can hurt the value of a quilt. Others wash their quilts all the time.

CHARACTERISTICS OF SYNTHETIC BATTS

- Resists wrinkling when quilts are stored.
- Stands up to repeated launderings.
- Little, if any, shrinkage.
- Some topical treatments can trigger people's allergies.
- Lighter in weight than cotton.
- Microfiber batts are more breathable than other synthetic batts.
- Good choice for hand quilting and tying.

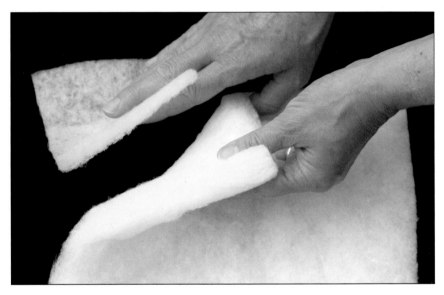

TIP

After a while, every quilter develops a fondness for a particular type of batting but this takes time. I encourage you to try different battings until you find one that suits the way you like to quilt. Ask at your local quilt shop for batting suggestions. Buy samples of different battings to try in small projects so that you can get a feel for their distinct qualities.

Make a Quilt Sandwich

Now that you have a complete top, a backing, and batting, you need to layer these three pieces into a quilt sandwich. Like many other aspects of quilting, a number of different ways are available to do this step. This is my favorite method for quilts larger than 3 × 5 feet. If your project is smaller than this, use a smaller working surface. The point is for the edges of your project to hang over two sides of your working surface and that its center is within easy reach.

① I know quilters who have used their sewing room floors, ping pong tables, and kitchen tables for this part of the quilting process. My favorite work surface for this activity, however, is a sturdy folding table, longer than it is wide, available in many department or office supply stores. They are easy to find in 3 × 5 or 3 × 6 feet. Mark the exact center of each side of the table by taping a toothpick to mark this location.

Note: Tape toothpicks or drinking straw sections where you mark the center of the table so you can feel the centering marks through the fabric and batting while you are adjusting the layers.

② Fold your backing in half across its width, right side out to find its center. Mark this location on both sides of the backing with pins. Unfold the backing.

③ Now fold the backing across its length, right side out, to find its center. Mark this location on both sides of the backing with pins. Keep the backing folded.

Note: If your quilt is large, a second pair of hands is helpful to have when doing this part.

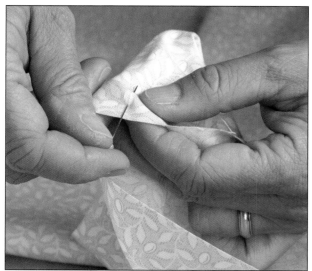

④ Drape your backing wrong side up and lengthwise over the width of your work table. The top and bottom edges of your backing should fall over the edges of your table as if the backing was a tablecloth.

⑤ Align the pins marking the centers of the length of your backing with the centering marks on the sides of your table. Gently smooth out any folds or wrinkles in your backing, being careful not to move it from its centered position.

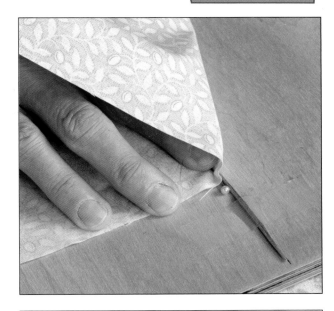

⑥ Cut your batting to the same size as your backing. Mark the centers of all four sides with pins, as you did the backing, then lay it on the table over the backing. Align the pins marking the centers of all four sides of the batting with the pins marking the centers of the backing. Gently smooth and fluff the batting into place. If the batting has been rolled up for some time, it may resist lying flat. If this happens, let it stay in place overnight to relax.

CONTINUED ON NEXT PAGE

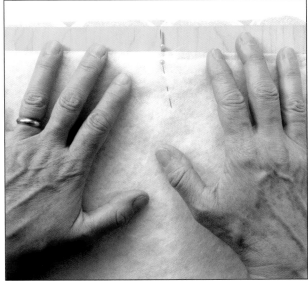

7 Fold your quilt top as you did your backing, this time wrong side up, and mark its centers with pins as you did the backing and batting. Lay it on top of the batting, align the centers, and smooth as you have the other layers. Be very gentle with this action. You do not want to stretch any fabric.

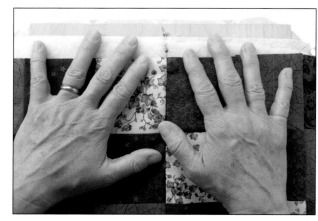

8 Your backing must be smooth and taut. If you have a helper to work with, stand on opposite sides of the table, reach under the layers to find the edge of the backing and gently pull on it at the same time. If you are working alone, firmly place one hand on the quilt top while pulling the backing taut with the other hand. Work along both sides in this fashion until the backing is smooth.

TIP

Move your hands in a sweeping motion over your quilt sandwich as you pin and baste to make sure you eliminate folds, creases, and wrinkles. Never pull on your batting. It is not a woven material, so it can be pulled apart easily.

9. Starting in the center of the quilt top, insert a straight pin through all three layers. Insert a second pin approximately 3 inches to the left of your center pin. Move 3 inches to the right of the center pin to insert a third pin. Work back and forth in this manner down the center of the width of the quilt top. Hold the fabric sandwich firmly while you pin so that the layers don't slide over one another. The idea here is to secure the layers while encouraging any fabric folds or fluff in the batting to move out from the center toward the edges of the quilt. Pin so that the heads of your pins are always on the right (if right handed) or left (if left handed).

10. If you are going to tie the three layers of your quilt together, please turn to the beginning of Chapter 17 for further instructions on pinning and tying. If your project is a good choice to machine quilt-as-you-go, please turn to "Quilt as You Go" in Chapter 17. If you plan to hand quilt your project, please continue to the next section on pinning and basting.

TIP

Check and recheck to be sure the three layers of your quilt sandwich are smooth and taut as you pin and baste. Stop once in a while to inspect the back of your quilt sandwich to be sure there are no folds or wrinkles. Move the quilt gently as you do this.

Basting for Hand Quilting

Once you put a layer of batting between two layers of fabric, it's very easy for the fabric layers to shift and move while they are being sewn or tied together. Basting is a temporary way to keep the layers of a quilt sandwich from moving.

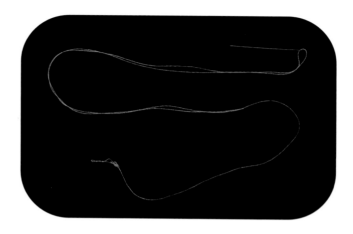

Basting Methods

There are many ways to baste a quilt. It can be done with straight pins as you tie a quilt together or machine quilt-as-you-go (see Chapter 17). You can purchase batting treated with an adhesive that's activated by the heat of an iron. This adhesive binds the three layers of a quilt together. If you learn how to machine quilt or take your project to a professional with a longarm quilting machine, the three layers of your quilt will be basted together with safety pins.

If you are going to quilt your project by hand (see Chapter 17), then hand basting is the best way to secure your quilt sandwich. There are several ways to accomplish this part of the quilting process. After some trial and error, this is the process I've developed.

NEEDLE AND THREAD BASTING

1. Basting stitches are running stitches, the simplest handsewing stitch of all. Generally speaking, keep your basting stitches small on the back side of your quilt, no more than ½ inch. Stitches visible on the top should be about 1½ to 2 inches long.

2. I pin and hand baste simultaneously while my quilt sandwich is on my work table. Following instructions for pinning the three layers of a quilt together in Step 9 in the previous section, complete four rows of pinning your quilt sandwich together. Your rows of pinning should be 2 to 3 inches apart. As you can see in this photo, your hand basting will be done between the rows of pins.

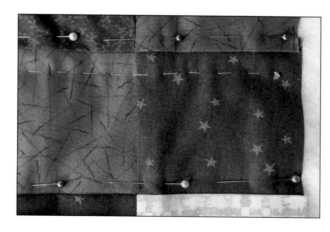

3 Thread your needle with 18 to 24 inches of thread. Knot the last end to come from the spool. Start sewing at the side of the quilt that matches your preferred sewing hand. Your first row of basting will be approximately one inch below your first row of pins. Stitch across the quilt through all three layers.

End your basting line with one or two back stitches. To back stitch, repeat the last stitch one or two times. This secures the end of the thread while making it easy to removed the basting when it is no longer needed.

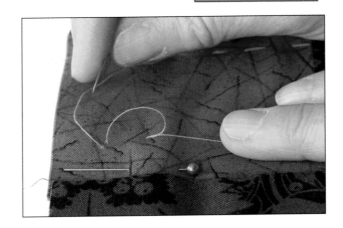

4 Once you finish the first row of basting, start a second row approximately 1 inch below your second row of pins. When you complete the second row of basting, gently slide your quilt sandwich away from you about 4 inches. Following instructions for pinning in Step 9 in the previous section, add two rows of pins to your quilt sandwich. Sew two rows of basting between your third and fourth rows of pins. Continue in this fashion until you reach the edge of the quilt. The idea is to always have two rows of pins ahead of your rows of basting.

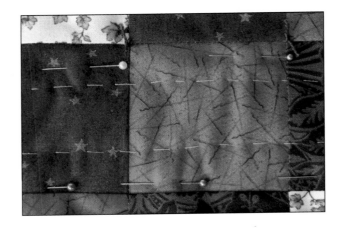

5 When you've pinned and basted to the first edge of your quilt, return to the quilt's center to pin and baste to the opposite edge. Once you have pinned and basted the length of your quilt, gently turn it over and take a look at the back to make sure it is smooth. Turn the quilt right side up. Turn the quilt so that it is lengthwise on your work table. Starting in the center and working toward the outside corners of the quilt, stitch a line of basting along the lengthwise edge. Turn the quilt and stitch a line of basting along the second lengthwise edge. It is very important to secure all four edges of your quilt sandwich with a line of basting as close to the outside of the quilt top as possible.

Potholders

Potholders and hot pads are among my favorite small quilting projects. Their diminutive size gives you a chance to experiment with color or pattern while making something useful. I also recycle blocks that don't come out quite right into potholders and hot pads (see "A Word about Squareness" in Chapter 12). So why do I have a section on potholders in this chapter? Because batting is an important component when making potholders.

Batting Safety

A number of quilted project patterns for items such as potholders, hot pads, tea cozies, and casserole carriers require safety considerations when it comes to batting. *Please, never use batting with synthetic fibers in any quilt project that is supposed to protect you from heat.* Synthetic fibers melt when in contact with high heat, which means your hands will not be protected.

The very best—and safest—batting to use in a potholder, hot pad, or casserole carrier is terrycloth towels or wash cloths. They are 100% cotton, widely available, and if used in a double layer, will protect your hands. It's also a great way to get more use out of an old towel.

TIP

Make sure that the thread you use to make potholders is also all cotton. If you tie your potholders or hot pads, be sure your tying material is also cotton.

Potholder Instructions

1 Make a single block using your favorite quilt pattern. Generally speaking, a good finished size for a potholder is 8 inches so your block should measure 8½ × 8½ inches. Cut a piece of back fabric 10 × 10 inches. Cut two pieces of terry-cloth (a used towel that's not too worn works well for this).

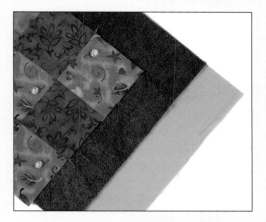

2 On your worktable, lay the backing fabric wrong side up. Layer both pieces of terrycloth, and then the potholder's top (right side up) to make this small quilt sandwich. Smooth each layer to remove folds and wrinkles as you lay them down.

3 Holding the layers carefully in place, pin them together, working from the center of the potholder to the outer edges. Before proceeding, turn the potholder over to be sure there are no wrinkles held in place by the pins. Repin if necessary. Once the pins are in place, stitch around the outside edges of the piece.

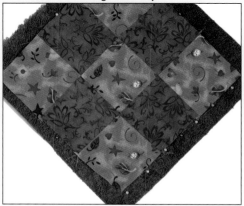

4 Because the multiple layers of batting make it difficult to quilt, I recommend tying the layers together, following instructions in Chapter 17. When tied, trim the batting and backing to the size of the top. Bind following instructions in Chapter 18.

chapter 17

Tying and Quilting

To many quilters, the whole point of piecing a quilt top is the opportunity to quilt. While the term *quilting* is used to refer to every part of this craft, the actual definition of *quilting* is stitching two pieces of fabric together in a three-part sandwich that includes a layer of batting in the middle. In many respects, this finishing process should be part of the preliminary planning for a quilt project. Your choices here have an impact on your choice of batting and, perhaps, even the pattern you choose to piece.

Of the choices presented here, tying is the quickest way to finish a quilt and it can add one more design element to a project. Technically, when you tie the three layers of a quilt together, the result is called a *comforter.* The batting in a comforter is usually high loft so that the finished project looks puffy. But I've tied quilt projects such as place mats and wall hangings with low-loft batting with satisfactory results.

Hand quilting takes more time, but I encourage you to try it. It is an invitation into the slowing of life that's so much a part of other crafts such as knitting, spinning, crocheting, and embroidery. You also have a lot of control over a quilt pattern because sewing by hand is so flexible. Machine quilting, however, is becoming more and more popular. In fact, many quilt shops as well as other professionals now offer machine-quilting services on specialized machines called *long arms.* You can also try this for yourself. I suggest you start your hand quilting experience with a small project or you can machine quilt a larger project using the quilt-as-you-go technique.

Tying

There are two ways to secure the three layers of a quilt together—tying or sewing by hand or machine.

Tying quilts is quicker and easier than hand or machine quilting. Plus, if you play with the color of your tying material, you get to add one more design element to your project.

TOOLS AND SUPPLIES

In order to tie a quilt project, you need a darning needle and one of the following: wool or synthetic worsted-weight yarn, perle cotton, crewel embroidery yarn, knitting cotton, or embroidery floss. Thread, no matter how heavy, is not appropriate for tying a quilt project.

QUILTING DISTANCE

Look closely at a comforter and you'll see that its ties appear at regular intervals across its length and width. The quilt top pattern and the choice of batting determines the length of this interval, which is called the *quilting distance* and ranges between 2 and 6 inches.

When planning your tying pattern, look for places in your top that occur at regular intervals and measure between them to be sure you can accommodate your quilting distance. In the photo, the finished size of the squares is 3 × 3 inches and the quilting distance of the low loft polyester batting is 2–4 inches. Placing a tie at each corner of each square stabilizes the batting and emphasizes design elements in the quilt's top.

Note: *If you buy batting by the bag, the quilting distance is marked on the bag. If you buy batting by the yard, ask what the quilting distance is.*

TIE YOUR QUILT

1 There are several ways to prepare quilts for tying. Stretch out large, bed-sized projects on frames that hold the quilt sandwich taut while it is tied, or lay them out on a large table where you can fully baste (see Chapter 16) and tie them. You can pin and tie smaller projects—twin-size bed quilts and less—simultaneously.

Note: Quilts used for bedspreads come in the following sizes: twin: 74 × 102 inches; double: 88 × 102 inches; queen: 97 × 125 inches; king: 111 × 111 inches.

2 Make your quilt sandwich (see Chapter 16). Starting in the center of the top, insert a pin through all three layers. Insert a second pin 3 inches to the left of the center pin. Move 3 inches to the right of the center pin to insert a third pin. Work back and forth across the width of your quilt sandwich until you have six rows of pins. Make sure you insert the pins with their heads toward the center of the quilt.

3 Your tie color can contrast, complement, or blend with the fabric (I used a contrasting perle cotton). Thread the needle with at least 18 inches of tying material. Start at your first pin and push your needle through all three layers of the quilt (a).

Pull through all three layers, leaving a 3-inch tail of thread on top. Turn the needle around and come back through all three layers close to where you began. Pull the thread just snug to the back of the quilt (b).

4 Quilters have developed several different knots for tying quilts. I use a double knot, often called a Granny knot. To make the first part of this double knot, hold one tail of your tie in each hand. Cross the right over the left so the ties are in an X shape. Wind the right tail away from you, down through the bottom part of the X and then up toward you. Tighten the knot to the quilt top.

CONTINUED ON NEXT PAGE

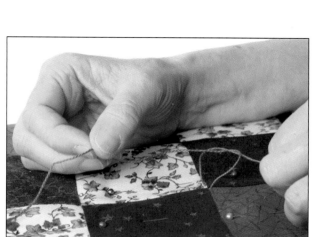

⑤ Hold the tails of the tie as before and repeat Step 4.

⑥ Once the knot is tight against the quilt top, clip the tails so they are no more than ½ to 1 inch long. Move toward your sewing hand to your next tie location and continue tying until you are within your quilting distance of the edge of the quilt. Do not tie any closer than 1 inch from the edge of your quilt to leave room to sew on your binding.

Move to the opposite side of your work table. Start in the center and tie toward the opposite side of your quilt. Do not tie any closer than 1 inch from the edge of your quilt to leave room to sew on your binding. Continue pinning and then tying your quilt until your quilt sandwich is fully secure.

⑦ Flip your project over to the back side and check to be sure there are no pucks or unwanted folds caught by ties in the backing. If there are, carefully cut just that tie and remove it then thread your needle and make a new tie in that place. When finished, ties should look like small stitches on the back of your quilt as you can see in this picture.

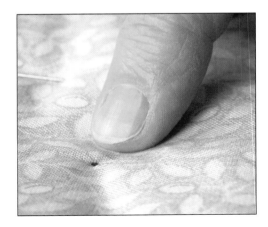

One of the benefits of hand quilting is that you don't have to lug a sewing machine around with you to do it. I suggest you start your hand quilting experience with a small project.

Hand quilting is not a complicated process but it does take some practice to get your stitches even. Generally speaking, if you set aside three to four hours to focus on this skill, you should settle into the rhythm of it.

CONTINUED ON NEXT PAGE

Hand quilting requires the following tools:

- **Needles** in the size referred to as *betweens.* This type of needle is small enough to let you make smaller stitches. If you're uncertain what size will suit you best, start with a size 9 or 10. Many quilt shops carry needles made specifically for quilting and these are worth the purchase price because they're made stronger to withstand the stress of repeatedly piercing two layers of fabric and batting.

- **Thimble.** A good choice is a metal thimble with a dimpled, flat top. Many people find it difficult to get used to sewing with a thimble and several alternatives are on the market. One way to get used to a thimble is to wear it around the house as you do other chores so that your middle finger (the one that pushes the needle through the fabric) grows accustomed to this important sewing tool.

- **Sharp scissors.** These are a must for cutting thread. If you have a habit of misplacing them, try tying a long piece of ribbon through one of the handles and wearing them around your neck—if the blades will stay closed.

- **Needle threader.** If you have trouble threading a needle, this should do the trick.

- **Thread.** Remember that your quilting stitches will show on both sides of your quilt so choose your thread carefully, making sure it's cotton thread. If you want to maximize your stitching, choose a neutral colored thread that will show dark on your light fabrics and light on your darks. Or you may choose to change the color of your thread to match your fabrics.

- A **quilter's hoop** is not the same as an embroidery hoop; it is wider, approximately 2 inches, and can be tightened by a screw arrangement. Choose a hoop that will fit comfortably in your lap or you may want to investigate a hoop with an attachment that fits under your legs in order to free your hands. Floor-stand hoops are also available.

- Other quilting tools include a **pincushion** to keep your needles at the ready, **narrow masking tape** to make temporary straight lines to guide your sewing, and a **mechanical pencil** and **ruler** to make grid lines.

TIP

No matter how hard I try, I cannot sew with a thimble. But I still need to protect the part of my finger that pushes a needle through cloth. Small leather circles, like the one pictured here, have adhesive on the back and can be reused several times. I use them with great success. Be aware that they will not stick to your skin right after you use hand lotion.

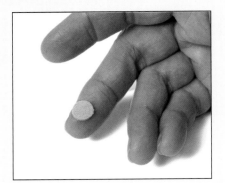

Each of the five quilt projects in the following section features a different quilting pattern. Some are examples of straight-line quilt stitch patterns while others feature other pattern options.

Before you begin to quilt, carefully consider how your stitching will impact the pattern you've established with your quilt blocks and what you would like to emphasize in your finished quilt.

Five Quilting Patterns

1 This type of quilting is called *stitch in a ditch*. The quilting stitches lie, literally, directly in or right next to the seam lines. In this case, the shape of the fabric squares is emphasized by quilting only two lines—one vertical, one horizontal—from side to side and top to bottom. This example uses quilting to enhance a simple block pattern.

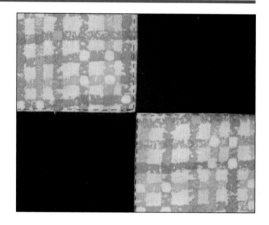

2 You can add directionality to a simple pattern by quilting in a grid that overlaps in the center of each square. Visually, this type of quilt pattern makes quarter-square triangles out of simple squares.

CONTINUED ON NEXT PAGE

③ This diamond grid is actually a stitched square set on point. It overlaps the triangles in the block and adds another layer of interest to a quilt top.

④ In addition to grids and stitch-in-a-ditch quilting, you can add interest to a quilt block's pattern by using it as your quilting pattern as well. Or you can stitch around elements in the print of a fabric. These are both called *outline quilting.* Both types are in this Ohio Star example. The quilting on the right follows lines made by the four parts of the quarter square triangle. On the left, the quilting follows the shape of the stars in the fabric.

⑤ You can add interest to a fabric block with stand-alone quilt motifs such as these hearts. This is a simple form of a technique called *trapunto.*

Quilting without a hoop or frame—often called *lap quilting*—is perfect for small projects that you can hold in your hands. You can also hand quilt using a hoop or a frame. Before you thread a needle, you need to decide how you want to quilt your project. The instructions below cover the basics of the hand quilting process. As you advance in this technique, I encourage you to explore the many stitching designs available to the hand quilter.

CHOOSE YOUR QUILT DESIGN

If you decide to quilt your project with a pattern that does not use one of the techniques described below, then you need to mark your pattern on your top before you make your quilt sandwich. For light fabrics, use a mechanical pencil with a #2 lead. Anything softer will smudge. For dark fabrics, use a chalk pencil. If you are using pencil, make your lines light. No matter what type of marker you use, make sure the point is kept sharp as you mark.

To guide your stitching just outside a seam, lay one edge of ¼-inch masking tape on the seam line with the opposite edge marking the line you wish to stitch. You can also use tape to help you stitch across blocks in the diagonal. *Be careful to never leave tape on fabric for long periods of time because its adhesive will stay on your fabric.*

Note: *Available in quilt shops, a narrow tape called quilter's tape comes in ¼ and ⅛-inch widths.*

> ## TIP
>
> There are hundreds of curved and intricate quilting patterns available in quilt shops, magazines, and online. Once you're comfortable with straight-line hand quilting, I urge you to experiment with these more intricate patterns.

1 Before you start to quilt, baste your project following instructions in Chapter 16. To begin quilting, cut a length of thread 18–24 inches long and thread your needle. You are going to stitch with a single strand of thread. Do not knot the end of your thread.

2 There are a few ways to begin and end a line of quilt stitching. I like the backstitch method. Insert the tip of your needle through the quilt top and into the batting. Do not go through the backing. Maneuver the point of your needle in the direction of your quilting line approximately 1 inch away from your starting point.

3 Push the tip of the needle out of the quilt top. Gently pull on your thread just until its end disappears inside your quilt sandwich.

4 Move the needle's point ¼ inch toward the starting point. Insert the point into the quilt top and batting and make a small backstitch. The point should re-emerge near the same hole you made in Step 3.

5 Re-insert your needle into the hole you made at the beginning of this step and come out where you started in Step 3. Do not pierce the backing during this backstitch sequence.

6 With your sewing hand on top and other hand underneath, push the needle through all three layers where you wish to begin quilting. When you feel the point of the needle on the back side of the quilt, turn the needle back up. As soon as it appears on top, turn it so it heads back down again. Do this back-and-forth motion until you have 3 or 4 equal stitches on the needle. Pull it through the top layer until the thread lays flat. Continue to the end of your thread.

7 You end a row of quilting the same way you began, with a back stitch. To hide the end of your thread, insert the point of your needle through the quilt top and into the batting. Maneuver your needle away from your final back stitch approximately one inch, then push your needle through the top. Cut the thread as close to the fabric as possible without cutting the fabric.

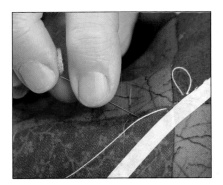
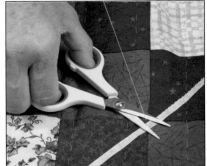

8 Many hand quilters use a hoop to hold their work as they stitch. Some hoops have attachments that slide under a quilter's legs so that both hands are free to sew. There are also hoops with attachments that rest on the floor. You can also use a hoop that you can hold in your hand. Don't pull your quilt as tight as a drum, but give it some flexibility while it is in the hoop so that you can rock your needle back and forth while quilting.

Note: *Do not leave your work in a hoop when you are not working on it.*

Machine Quilt As You Go

The quilt-as-you-go method is a good introduction to the machine quilting process and can be accomplished without special attachments for your sewing machine. It is perfect for projects that are the size of a twin bed or smaller. It uses the same technique as the sew-and-flip method of crazy quilting used in Chapter 15. Select quilt projects without borders such as the place mats in Chapter 7 or the Pinwheel Star quilt in Chapter 13 for quilt as you go.

This Pinwheel Star quilt was quilted using the quilt-as-you-go method. There are no ties or quilting stitches visible on its top. Use only low-loft batting for this method of quilting.

1 Following instructions in Chapter 16, cut your backing and batting, and make your quilt sandwich. Orient your quilt top so that the seams you made to put your rows together are horizontal as you look at the quilt, not vertical.

2 You are going to secure the three layers of your quilt together along its left and right edges. Starting at the center of your left edge, pin the three layers of your quilt together from the center of the quilt to its bottom corner. Do the same to the right edge.

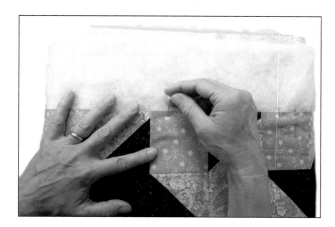

③ Flip the unpinned half of your quilt top wrong-side up so the row seam in the center of your quilt is exposed. Smooth the seam against the batting. Make sure your backing is taut. Lightly pin (2–3 inch intervals) the exposed seam to the batting and backing.

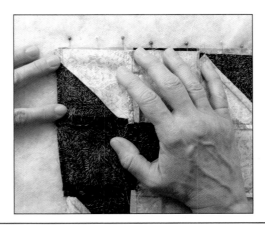

④ Lessen the tension of the top thread on your sewing machine a little. (See your owner's manual for instructions.) Guide your quilt so that your machine repeats the original seam you made for this row. You will have two rows of overlapping stitching as in this picture.

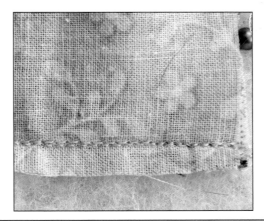

⑤ Flip the unpinned half of the quilt top right-side up. Place one hand on top of the quilt. With the other, gently pull on the backing to make it smooth and taut. Smooth out the batting if necessary but do not pull on it. Flip the quilt top wrong-side up again, folding it at the next row up from the seam you just stitched. Follow steps 3 and 4 above to sew this seam.

⑥ Set your iron to a low heat. Working on the quilt's top, lightly press each seam open as it is sewed. Do not move your iron back and forth but up and down. Watch the heat carefully. If you are using polyester batting, a too-hot iron can melt it.

CONTINUED ON NEXT PAGE

7 Once you have quilted-as-you-go over the first half of your project, unpin the other side. Start one row from your center seam (already stitched) and quilt-as-you-go down the second half of your quilt, following the instructions in steps 3–6 on previous page. Stop from time to time to check the seams on the back of your quilt. They should not have any folds or wrinkles in them.

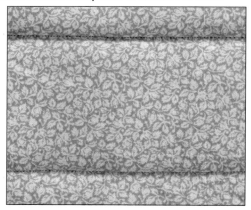

8 When you have finished quilting your whole project, trim the excess batting and backing from the left and right sides of your project, following instructions at the beginning of Chapter 18. This photo is of the left side of the Pinwheel Star quilt after it was trimmed. You can see where the stitching holds the batting between the top and backing.

9 Hand baste or machine stitch the bottom and top edges of your quilt together. If you machine stitch, lessen the tension in your top thread to help prevent the top fabric from sliding over the batting as you sew. Trim the excess batting and backing off after you have stitched the edges. Proceed to Chapter 18 to bind your project.

10 You can add trapunto effects to your quilt once it is secure with quilt-as-you-go. I used shapes cut from foam that I found in a craft store as templates and traced a dotted line around them, then hand quilted the designs following instructions earlier in this chapter.

As machine quilting has grown in popularity, a number of sewing-machine manufacturers have developed long arm machines to accommodate large projects. These machines can be quite a financial investment. A number of quilt shops and quilting professionals offer long arm quilting services for large quilt projects. This may be a better option for you than doing it yourself.

Photo courtesy of Gammill Quilting Machine Company.

chapter 18

Binding

Binding is the final stage of quilting, and for that reason, it is perhaps one of the most satisfying parts of quilt making. When you make that last stitch to secure your binding to the outer edge of your quilted creation, you finally see all of the choices you've made come together.

Like almost every other aspect of quilting, choosing the fabric for your binding gives you another chance to play with color. This chapter covers how to secure the outer edges of your quilt in a binding that complements your previous color selections. It also shows you ways to determine the length of binding necessary to finish a quilt and two methods of creating continuous binding strips.

Prepare Quilt for Binding

Of all the parts of a quilt, the binding is the one most subject to wear and tear because it is handled more than any other part of a quilt. Therefore, be extra careful on this final step so that the outer edge of your finished piece is as durable as possible. You'll start by evening up the edges of your quilted piece. I chose to illustrate the binding process using some of the place mat projects from Chapter 6 so that you can easily see the progression of the steps in this chapter.

① Find a space large enough to hold your finished piece. Lay it flat, top side up, and smooth it out with sweeping motions of your hands, beginning in the center and moving toward the outer edges (a).

② If you have not done so, hand- or machine-stitch the edges of your quilt sandwich on all four sides. Stitch as close to the outside edge of your top as possible.

③ Using your mat, rotary cutter, and wide ruler, trim off excess batting and backing so that all three layers of the quilt are even with one another. When you are done with this step, take the time to lay a corner of your ruler in each of the four corners of your quilt to make sure its corners are square. Then measure the outside dimensions of your quilt on all four sides. Note these dimensions on a piece of paper for later use.

Note: *If your project is too large to fit on a mat, place the mat under one corner of your project, cut off the excess batting and backing, then move the mat and continue cutting. As you do this, make sure the quilt stays flat.*

Continuous binding strips are by far my favorite way to make a binding for a quilt. A *continuous binding strip* is a ribbon of fabric long enough to bind a whole quilt. This type of binding is rugged, easy to attach once you get the hang of it, and handles corners well. Plus, it's versatile enough to allow for a multicolored binding if you wish.

Determine Fabric Measurements and Colors

1 You already completed part of this step when you measured the outer dimensions of your quilt. Now add these four measurements together and add 15 inches to the total. This extra 15 inches allows for turning corners and for the binding's finish. The total represents the length of fabric strips you will need to bind your quilt.

Note: Generally speaking, I cut my binding strips 2½ inches wide on the crosswise grain of my chosen fabric. When finished, this width yields a binding that's ½ inch wide on both the front and back of the quilt. Adjust your width accordingly if you want a narrower or wider binding. Continuous binding strips may also be cut to full length on the lengthwise grain of fabric. This choice requires longer pieces of fabric.

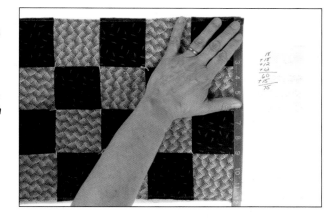

2 Before you cut your binding strips, take a moment to consider your color choice. Each of the place mats pictured features a different choice. The one on the left uses the lighter color in the top for the binding, the middle piece uses the darker color, and the one on the right combines the two. Note the different visual impacts these bindings have on the finished project. Audition your fabric choices before you sew to see which pleases your eye the best.

CONTINUED ON NEXT PAGE

Cut and Sew Continuous Binding Strips

1 In general, each strip of cloth cut crosswise from fabric yardage yields a length of 40 inches. To determine how many strips you need for your binding, take the total of your measurements of the outside of your quilt plus the extra 15 inches and divide that total by 40. The answer, rounded up to the next whole number, will be the number of strips you need to cut to bind your quilt.

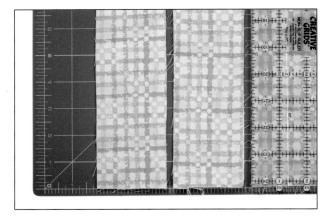

2 Take two of your strips and cross them over one another as pictured, right sides together. You are going to sew them together diagonally so place pins so they hold the fabric pieces together but are out of sewing range (a).

3 Where the two strips cross, sew them together with a diagonal seam running from the top left corner to the bottom right corner (b).

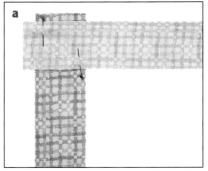
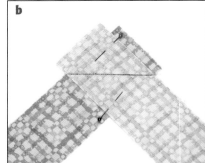

4 Once the seam is complete, cut off the excess fabric ¼ inch to the right of the seam. Press the seam open.

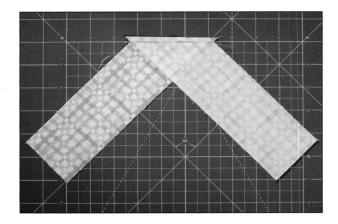

5 When pressed open, the diagonal seams between binding strips will look like this picture. As with triangles, cut off tabs of excess fabric. Continue sewing strips to one another to the desired length of your binding.

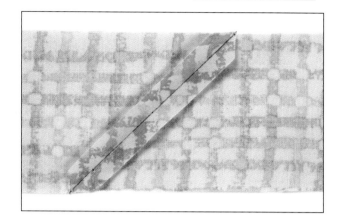

6 If you wish to make a multi-colored binding, cut a number of fabric strips from your chosen fabrics to equal the total you need to bind your quilt plus another 15–20 inches to cover the seam allowances. When I create a multi-colored binding, I cut the longer strips into shorter lengths before I sew them together so that the color will change continuously around the quilt.

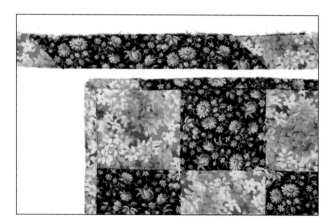

TIP

The color choices for binding are not limited to the fabrics in your quilt. In fact, a quilt may benefit from a binding that is not part of the quilt top. The Pinwheel Star quilt in Chapter 13 is a good example of a quilt that is enhanced by a binding of a color not in the quilt top. So take time to test a variety of fabrics for this part of your quilt.

Bias Binding Strips

I use binding strips cut across the crossgrain for all of my quilts with one exception. I like the look of striped fabric bindings much better if they are cut on the bias. This across-the-grain cutting technique yields a binding that gives the illusion that the stripes are winding around the outside of the quilt.

Quilting Math

1 Bias bindings are cut from a single square of fabric. There's some math involved with this calculation and it's easier with a calculator. Carefully measure the top, bottom, and side dimensions of your quilt. Add these measurements together and add 8 inches. Multiply this result by the width of your binding, 2½ inches in this case. This calculation gives you the area of the binding. Now grab a calculator and find the square root of this sum. This result, in inches, gives you the dimension of the square of fabric that you need for your bias binding. Round up to the nearest whole inch.

2 Let's use this placemat as an example. It measures 18 inches on top and bottom (for a total of 36) and 12 inches on each side (for a total of 24). When you add 8 inches to the total of these dimensions, the total is 68. Multiply this by 2.5 for 170 (the area of the binding). The square root of this number is 13.03. I find rounding up to the nearest inch is a good habit, so the square for this bias is 14 × 14 inches.

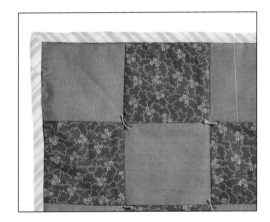

3 Cut a square of fabric to your final dimension.

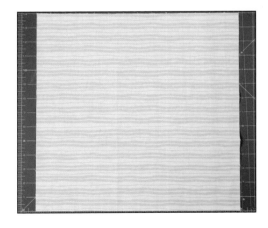

④ Cut the square diagonally, just as you do when you make half-square triangles.

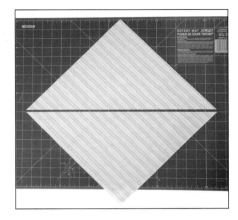

⑤ Take one of the triangles and turn it over so that the right sides of the fabric are facing one another and the triangles are lying on one another as pictured. Sew the triangles together along the edge that they have in common. Press the seam open.

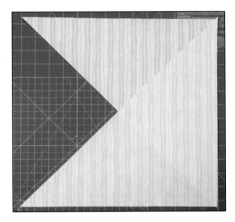

⑥ Lay your binding on your cutting mat so that the bottom edge is even with a measuring line on the mat.

CONTINUED ON NEXT PAGE

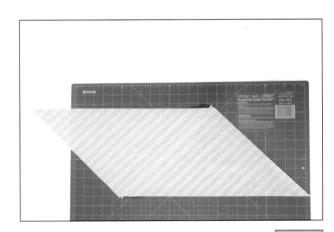

7 Measure across 2½ inches and cut a strip of fabric. Continue in this fashion across the fabric. If the final piece is less than 2½ inches, remove this piece.

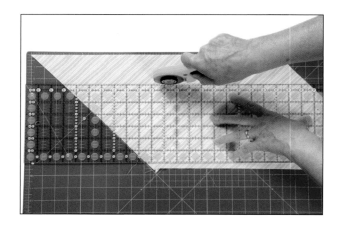

8 The ends of each piece of fabric that you cut should be angled, as pictured.

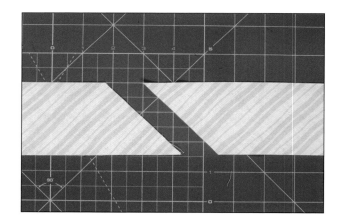

9 Lay one fabric strip on top of another, with right sides together. Make sure the leading points of each strip overhang the outside edges of the strips. Stitch all the strips together in this way, pressing the seams open. When the strips are sewn together, take your scissors and cut off these leading points as you would when you sew half-square triangles (see Chapter 13). When you are done, you will have a single ribbon of bias-cut binding for your quilt project. Be sure to handle bias-cut binding gently because it is very stretchy.

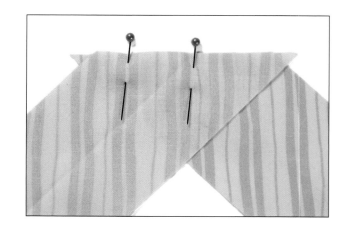

The best way to hang a quilt or quilted wall hanging is via a sleeve of fabric attached to the back. This needs to be added to your quilt before the binding is attached.

---

1 If you intend to hang your quilt project, decide which side of it will be at the top when it is hanging. Measure the quilt along this side and subtract two inches. Cut a strip of fabric 4 inches wide and to this measurement. Turn the raw edges of both ends under and stitch them in place.

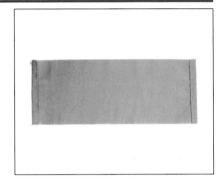

2 Lay your sleeve, right side up, on the back of your quilt with the top edge of the sleeve aligned with the top edge of your quilt. Pin in place. Turn the quilt face up and attach the binding (see the following section for full instructions). When you attach your binding to the top of your quilt, your sleeve will be included in that stitching.

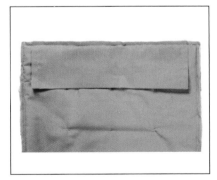

3 When the binding is stitched into place, turn the raw edge of the bottom of the sleeve under (use an iron to press this into place) and pin it to the back of the quilt. Using thread to match the back or sleeve, hand sew the bottom of the sleeve to the quilt's backing only. Do not stitch through to the front of the quilt.

Note: *When you want to hang your quilted project, slide a curtain rod through the sleeve.*

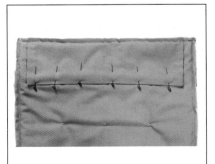

Attach Binding Strips

When you attach your binding to the front of your quilt, you will sew through four layers of fabric and a layer of batting. Be sure the needle in your machine is in good condition and sew slowly for best results. Before you sew on your binding, sew or handstitch all three layers of your quilt together around the outside edges.

1 Cut one end of bias strip to a 45° angle (close, not exact). Turn edge in ¼ in. and press into place. Fold strip in half lengthwise, (right side of fabric on outside), and press along whole length.

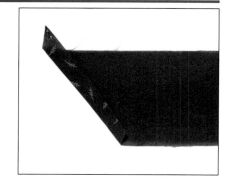

2 Locate the middle of one side of the quilt and lay one end of binding there. Align the open side of the binding strip with the quilt edge. Pin the binding to the front of the quilt (push pins through all three layers), leaving the first 6 inches of the beginning of the binding strip unpinned.

3 Start your first seam 6 inches from the beginning of the binding. Continue sewing until you are ¼ inch from your first corner. Backstitch to make the end of the seam secure. Cut the thread and pull the project from the machine. Lay it on a firm surface.

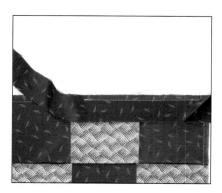

4 You're now going to make a fold in the binding at each corner of your project. This fold allows the fabric to ease over the corner in much the same way a dart eases fabric around the curve of a body so clothing will fit. First, fold the binding away from the project and perpendicular to it.

5 Place your finger on the binding to hold it in place, then fold it down in alignment with the next side.

6 Pin the binding to the second side.

CONTINUED ON NEXT PAGE

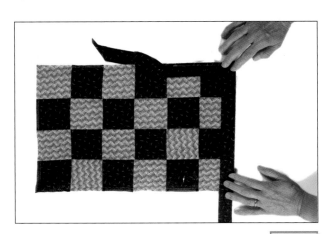

7 Stitch the binding to the second side, starting right at the beginning of the seam and stopping ¼ inch from the end. Backstitch, cut the threads, and remove the project from the sewing machine. Fold the fabric at the corner as you did before. Attach binding to the third side, fold the fabric at the corner, and stitch down the fourth side until you near the place where you began.

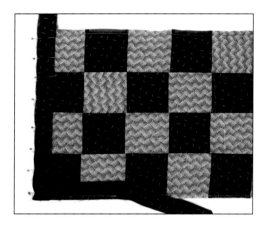

8 Stop stitching about 3 inches before the loose binding you left at the beginning of this process. Align the loose beginning of the binding with the edge of the project. Cut the tail end of the binding so that there is a 3-inch overlap of the beginning and end of the binding.

9 Think of the beginning of your binding—the portion not stitched to the quilt—as a pocket. Align its top edge with the edge of your quilt. Open it with your fingers and maneuver the loose end of your binding into this pocket so that the fit is as snug as you can make it. Pin this whole section to the project carefully, making sure all layers are pinned together and that there are no wrinkles or folds in the binding. Sew this last part of the binding into place.

You are finally at the very last step of quilt making, which is hand stitching the binding to the back of your quilt project.

Turn, Pin, and Stitch the Binding

1 Turn your project face down and gently turn the binding toward the back of your quilt. In the photograph, note how the fold that you made in the binding forms around each corner of the quilt.

2 Working on one side at a time, pin the binding in place to the back of the quilt. When you reach a corner, tuck the excess of the fold to the right (a), then overlap it by folding the remaining fabric to the left (b).

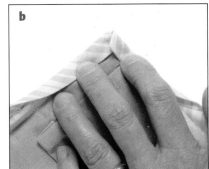

3 Working with the smallest needle that you can handle comfortably, whip stitch the binding to the back of the quilt. Be careful not to let your stitches come through to the front. I usually take some extra stitches at the corners for reinforcement. End your stitching with a couple of back stitches, and then cut the thread.

Congratulations! You've completed a quilt!

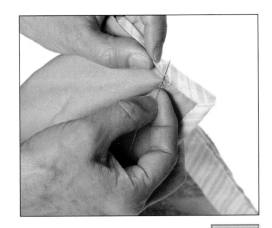

Appendix: Quilt Gallery

Once a year, the members of the Ladies Circle of Pomfret, Vermont, make a quilt to be raffled off at the town's annual harvest celebration. The raffle's proceeds are used for scholarships and to support community projects. This quilt top's block pattern is called Bear's Claw, a combination of squares and half-square triangles. Sashing and posts surround each block and the top is finished with a double border. In order to tie the quilt, the members set up a frame of four wooden rails, tack the edges of the muslin backing to the rails, roll out a layer of batting, and then stretch out the quilt's top. As the tying proceeds, the layered quilt is rolled up on one of the rails, working from top to bottom, until the entire quilt is tied. This type of communal activity has been part of the quilting culture in this country since colonial times.

This magnificent crazy quilt was made by the members of the Northern Lights Quilters guild, based in Lebanon, New Hampshire, to celebrate the wedding of member Nellie Pennington of South Strafford, Vermont. Before the blocks were made, the makers chose a single fabric—in this case, an oriental print—to be the common element in every block. Other than the common fabric, every block was individualized by its maker. Crazy quilting began in Victorian England in the late nineteenth century, and many of its embroidered motifs have symbolic meaning. The spider and web, such as the ones pictured here in the detail, are symbols of good luck.

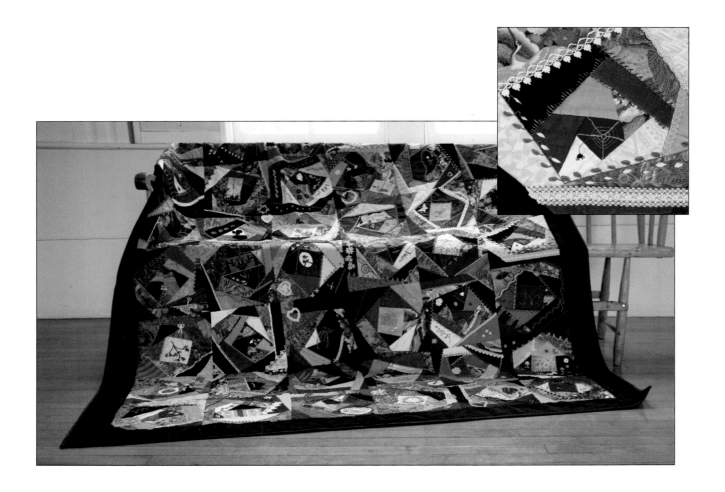

This quilt by Dori Galton of Hartland, Vermont, is a great example of how there's really nothing simple about the simple square. Dori chose fabrics in a narrow range from dark to light in reds and blues, arranging them so that the lightest ones became the centers of attention. Most of the fabrics in this quilt include the color black, a fact emphasized by Dori's choice to use black thread to quilt her project and her choice of black as one of the three fabrics bordering the quilt top. She also incorporated squares of fabric from the top into the quilt's backing, a detail of which is pictured here.

Instead of using several different light and dark fabrics in the four traditional Log Cabin blocks in these pillows, Sue Wheeler of West Lebanon, New Hampshire, used the same fabrics. Then she moved the visual center of the pillow to the dark fabrics by sewing the four blocks together with the dark logs abutting. But the centers of the Log Cabin blocks she made are actually the squares of yellow fabric (see detail) which she repeats in the pillow's border. This ability to create secondary levels of pattern in a quilt top gives Log Cabin and its many variations their enduring popularity.

Kathi Moreno of White River Junction, Vermont, used a variation of Log Cabin known as Courthouse Steps for this stunning quilt. In Courthouse Steps you add the same fabric to two parallel sides of the center instead of one side at a time as in the traditional Log Cabin. In the detail, notice that each block consists of four different fabrics. The block on the right has a predominately black fabric in the center and ends with one predominately white. The block on the left has a predominately white fabric in the center and predominately black on the outside. When set next to one another in the quilt top, your eye is encouraged to move from one block to another.

Vivian Moore of Sharon, Vermont, used a wide array of scrap fabrics from her stash and even some fabric she inherited from her mother for this quilt made of Roman Roads blocks. Vivian chose to bracket single strips of light fabric with two strips of dark, alternated the direction of each block, and then sewed them together in diagonal rows. In the detail, notice how Vivian used two scraps of light in the same strip in order to make it long enough to match the dark.

This quilt of Four Patch blocks, made by Marilyn Mason of Lebanon, New Hampshire, is a good example of the power of a neutral color in a quilt top. This quilt top pattern, called Kitty Corner, uses Four Patch blocks and alternate squares to create a diagonal pattern. Examine the detail to see how she did it. The abundance of the neutral fabric—an off-white with spatters of color on it—lets the small blocks of color in the Four Patch squares march across the quilt top.

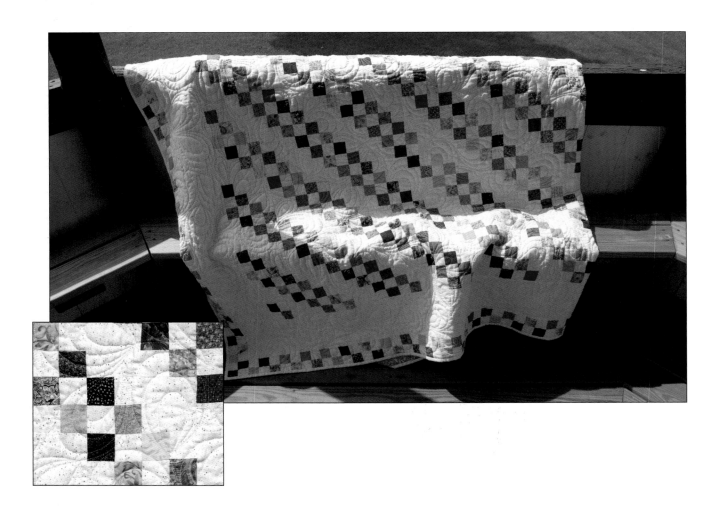

Because quilter Nancy Barr owns the Country Quilters Emporium in White River Junction, Vermont, she gets a fair number of fabric samples. This quilt started as a collection of 2½ inch sample squares, most of them replicas of fabrics popular in the 1930s. When she sat down to start sewing, Nancy put all of the samples in a paper bag and drew them out, one at a time, to sew the blocks in the center of the stars, a process she calls No-Peek Nine Patch. The bars of color that surround the stars are also Nine Patch blocks (see detail) with half-square triangles. Because the triangles were cut from 2⅞ inch squares, Nancy took that fabric from her stash.

LaVonne Batalden of Lebanon, New Hampshire, made this dramatic quilt to hang in her husband's office. The individual pieces in the top are squares, rectangles, and strips. LaVonne was inspired by a seeing a quilt with a similar pattern in a magazine and adapted the design. Once she had the pattern laid out, she sewed the top together in lengthwise strips. She machine stitched the quilt herself, using variegated thread (see detail).

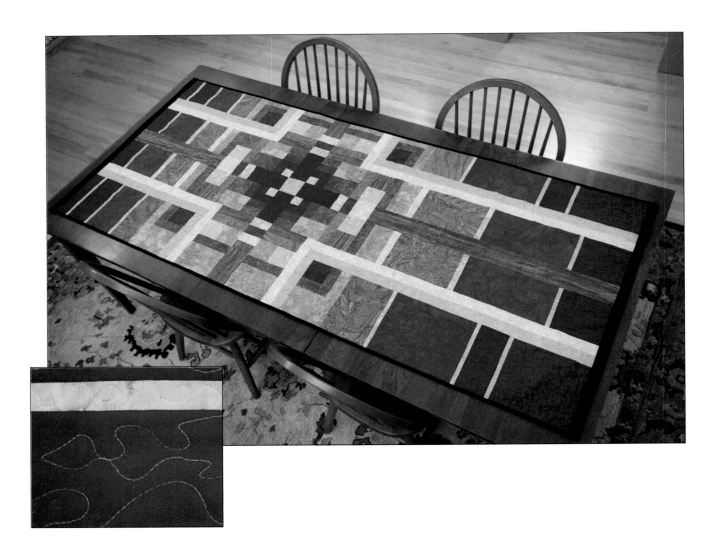

In October 2004, Barbara Vallone of Racine, Wisconsin, and two friends, Mary Bielefeldt and Pat Wolff, received donations of assorted scraps, odd squares, and yards of fabric and decided to hold a quilt workshop for charity. As Mary and Pat assembled the fabric donations into kits for the event, they combined oddball fabrics and squares into themes—Halloween, very bright fabrics, odd borders and border strips, Christmas—and filled brown paper lunch bags with their collections. Then they gave the numbered bags to Barbara, one at a time, to see what she could do with them. The result is a series of wall hangings and small quilts, three of which are here. Barbara set the pinwheels in this quilt off-center to enhance the design.

The red and green bow tie squares in the center of this quilt are set off by sashing and posts in three different widths starting in the center (see detail) and working out. Then the whole quilt top is surrounded by large triangles of a green Christmas print so that it is set on point.

Barbara fussy cut the six panels showing children at play on the front of this quilt from the novelty fabric that backs this quilt (see detail). The lower border on the front—the light blue with a string of red flowers—was also cut from the back fabric. Notice that the binding of this quilt is multi-colored. Barbara machine quilted each of these projects.

Linda Buzzell of Plainfield, New Hampshire, loves pinwheels. In this quilt, she juxtaposed her pinwheel blocks with half-square triangles to achieve a secondary pattern of diamonds. Each of her pinwheel blocks contains two pinwheels and two half-square triangles in the same two fabrics. Notice how she turned the half-square triangle units so that each block is visually cut in half on the diagonal. When four of these blocks are put together (see detail), they create a visual diamond. Linda also used pinwheels in the border of her quilt.

The diamond pattern in this quilt top begins in the center and moves out in ever larger diamond shapes. At first, it seems complicated but Ruth Ann Glick of White River Junction, Vermont, created this illusion with rows of half-square triangles that are light fabrics on one side and dark on the other. Examine the detail of the quilt and note that Ruth sewed her squares so that the dark fabrics are seamed together and the light are seamed together.

Joyce Lundrigan of Plainfield, New Hampshire, used a pattern called Sawtooth Star to make her star-within-a-star blocks for this quilt. Sawtooth Star is actually a square of fabric surrounded by four Flying Geese units. Joyce also used a variation of Roman Roads in this quilt, sewing two bars of similar fabrics—neutrals, greens, and blues—together to surround her Sawtooth Star blocks with color. The Flying Geese units are also repeated in the border.

As you grow as a quilter, I encourage you to seek out a quilt guild or join a group of people who enjoy quilting. Like the women pictured here from the Ladies Circle in Pomfret, Vermont—Elaine Chase, Miriam Desmond, Vivian Moore, Betty Stetson, and Gerda Gaetgens—joining a guild gives you a chance to enjoy this artful craft with others who enjoy creating beauty with fabric. Whatever you do in quilting, remember to enjoy yourself. That's the whole point.

Index

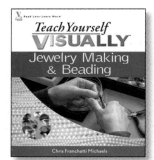
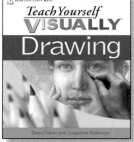